SERIAL KILLERS

Richard Ramirez

The Night Stalker

by Carla Mooney

Essential Library

An Imprint of Abdo Publishing
abdobooks.com

ABDOBOOKS.COM

Published by Abdo Publishing, a division of ABDO, PO Box 398166, Minneapolis, Minnesota 55439. Copyright © 2025 by Abdo Consulting Group, Inc. International copyrights reserved in all countries. No part of this book may be reproduced in any form without written permission from the publisher. Essential Library™ is a trademark and logo of Abdo Publishing.

Printed in China.
102024
012025

THIS BOOK CONTAINS RECYCLED MATERIALS

Cover Photo: Bettmann/Getty Images
Interior Photos: George Rose/Getty Images, 4–5; Elliott Cowand Jr/Shutterstock Images, 8; Felipe Caparros/Shutterstock Images, 10; ARCHIVIO GBB/Alamy, 12–13, 69; Sauer Jean-Claude/Paris Match/Getty Images, 16; Shutterstock Images, 18, 22–23, 36–37, 60; Hywit Dimyadi/Shutterstock Images, 27; Keith Birmingham/The Orange County Register/AP Images, 30; Creative Touch Imaging Ltd./NurPhoto/Getty Images, 32; Dan Lassiter/The Janesville Gazette/AP Images, 35; Irfan Khan/Los Angeles Times/Getty Images, 41; Bettmann/Getty Images, 45, 82; R. Krubner/ClassicStock/Getty Images, 48–49; Sonia Moskowitz/Getty Images, 53; Nick Ut/AP Images, 55, 85; Michael Goulding/The Orange County Register/AP Images, 56–57; Craig Golding/Fairfax Media/Getty Images, 64; Jeff Reinking/AP Images, 66–67; Steve Ringman/The San Francisco Chronicle/Getty Images, 71; Pierre Perrin/Gamma-Rapho/Getty Images, 73; Alan Zanger/Bettmann/Getty Images, 77; Lennox McLendon/AP Images, 78–79; Paul Harris/Getty Images, 90–91; Lacy Atkins/AP Images, 95

Editor: Arnold Ringstad
Series Designer: Joshua Olson

Library of Congress Control Number: 2024938310

PUBLISHER'S CATALOGING-IN-PUBLICATION DATA

Names: Mooney, Carla, author.
Title: Richard Ramirez: the night stalker / by Carla Mooney
Other title: the night stalker
Description: Minneapolis, Minnesota: ABDO Publishing, 2025 | Series: Serial killers | Includes online resources and index.
Identifiers: ISBN 9781098295370 (lib. bdg.) | ISBN 9798384916376 (ebook)
Subjects: LCSH: Ramirez, Richard Muñoz, 1960-2013--Juvenile literature. | Night Stalker, 1960-2013--Juvenile literature. | Killers (Murderers)--Biographies--Juvenile literature. | Serial killers--Biographies--Juvenile literature. | Crime--Juvenile literature. | True crime stories--Juvenile literature.
Classification: DDC 364.15232--dc23

CONTENTS

This book discusses accounts of crime, violence, and death that may be disturbing to some readers.

Chapter 1
A KILLING SPREE BEGINS 4

Chapter 2
A VIOLENT HOME 12

Chapter 3
ESCALATING VIOLENCE 22

Chapter 4
A CITY GRIPPED BY FEAR 36

Chapter 5
ATTACKS IN SAN FRANCISCO 48

Chapter 6
A BREAK IN THE CASE 56

Chapter 7
CAPTURING THE KILLER 66

Chapter 8
TRIAL AND CONVICTION 78

Chapter 9
LIFE AND DEATH BEHIND BARS 90

Essential Facts 100
Glossary 102
Additional Resources 104
Source Notes 106
Index 110
About the Author 112

CHAPTER 1

A KILLING SPREE BEGINS

On the night of March 17, 1985, Maria Hernandez was driving home on a Los Angeles, California, freeway after dinner with her boyfriend in Monterey Park. Hernandez exited the freeway into Rosemead, a residential suburb where she lived in a new condominium community. Shortly before 11:00 p.m., Hernandez pulled into the garage of the condo she shared with her roommate, 34-year-old Dayle Okazaki.

Hernandez gathered her keys and purse and stepped out of her car, moving toward an entry door in the garage. As she unlocked the door to the condo, Hernandez heard a sound. Hernandez recalled, "I turned around to see what the noise was. I saw a man; he was pointing a gun at me. . . . He started walking towards me."[1]

The man pointed his gun straight at Hernandez's head. Hernandez screamed and raised her hands. The man fired as the garage's automatic lights turned off.

The serial killer known as the Night Stalker terrorized Los Angeles and the surrounding area in the mid-1980s.

Hernandez said she felt "a cross between pain and heat on my right hand."[2] But miraculously, her keys had deflected the bullet. She fell to the ground. As Hernandez pretended to be dead, the man pushed her body out of his way and entered the condo.

With the man inside, Hernandez ran out of the garage. Unsure what to do and terrified for her friend, she approached the front of the condo. She heard a noise inside the condominium. Then she saw the man leaving the home. "I hid behind a car that was between us," Hernandez said. "He then noticed me and pointed the gun at me again. . . . I said, 'Please don't shoot me again.'"³ The man walked away.

After the man was gone, Hernandez entered the condominium. Her hand was bleeding and burning with pain. There, she found Okazaki lying face down on the kitchen floor with blood around her head. Hernandez shook Okazaki's shoulder and yelled her name, but there was no response. She ran upstairs to make sure there were no other intruders in the condo. Then she called the police.

Another Victim

Less than an hour after Okazaki's murder, Jorge Gallegos was sitting in a parked car with his girlfriend in front of her Monterey Park home. He noticed the sound of two

DAYLE OKAZAKI

Born in Hawaii, 34-year-old Dayle Okazaki was one of three siblings from a close family. She worked for Los Angeles County. Okazaki was well-liked by family and friends and always ready to lend a helping hand. For example, when a coworker talked about having to paint that weekend, Okazaki showed up Saturday morning with a paintbrush to help. On March 17, 1985, Okazaki watched a television movie with her parents before driving to her condo in Rosemead. It would be the last time anyone saw her alive.

cars slamming on their brakes. When Gallegos looked, it appeared as though one car had forced the other to the side of the road. Gallegos watched as a man got out of one car and pulled a struggling woman out of the other. The woman was 30-year-old law student Tsai-Lian "Veronica" Yu.

At the same time, Joseph Duenas heard the commotion from his home. He looked from his second-floor balcony and saw Yu struggling with a man. He went inside to call the police. When he returned to the balcony, Duenas watched the man push Yu to the ground and drive away. Yu crawled forward and then lay motionless.

When help arrived, Yu was unconscious but still alive. She had been shot twice in the chest. The paramedics raced her to the hospital. But by the time they got there, Yu had died.

Police Arrive

That same evening, March 17, Detective Gil Carrillo was watching television at home when he received a phone call. He learned that there had been a shooting at a condo. Carrillo was part of the Los Angeles Sheriff's Homicide Bureau. The detective had joined the Sheriff's Department

At the time of the killings, the Los Angeles Sheriff's Homicide Bureau investigated homicide cases in 64 of the 96 communities in the Los Angeles County area.

in 1971, but it was his first year working in the homicide group.

Carrillo arrived at the crime scene a little after midnight. He talked to the officers and studied the scene. Carrillo noticed a dark baseball hat with a logo from the rock band AC/DC on the garage floor. He left it to be processed by the crime scene unit. The crime scene unit's job was to preserve and categorize evidence. These specialists took photos and dusted for fingerprints. However, they found prints only from Hernandez and Okazaki.

At first, Carrillo thought the murder was the result of a love triangle. But after he spoke with Hernandez at the hospital, he was unsure. Hernandez insisted that she had no idea who the killer was. She had never seen him before and had no idea why he had targeted her and Okazaki. Carrillo believed her. He asked her to work with a sketch artist to create a picture of the killer.

Carrillo was getting a bad feeling about this case. He was starting to think the killer had chosen his victims at random. He believed that the man would try to kill again.

That same morning, forensic pathologist Dr. Susan Selser performed the autopsy of Tsai-Lian Yu. She removed the bullets from Yu's body and turned them over to detectives in Monterey Park as evidence. Later that day, ballistics testing reported that the bullets used to kill Okazaki and Yu had most likely come from the same gun. This suggested the same man had killed both women.

SKETCH ARTISTS

Sketch artists, also called forensic artists, help law enforcement by creating illustrations of suspects, missing persons, or victims. To create a sketch of a suspect, the artist talks to witnesses who provide verbal descriptions. The artist draws the suspect's face and other body parts from the verbal descriptions. When there are multiple witnesses, the artist combines the descriptions to create a composite sketch. The artist may use a pencil and paper or a digital tablet to create the drawing. The artist adjusts the drawing based on feedback from witnesses. Once finalized, the sketch can be used in the search for the suspect.

Investigators have been developing the science of forensic ballistics for more than a century.

Carrillo picked up the phone and called Sergeant Frank Salerno. Salerno was one of the best homicide detectives in the state, and Carrillo wanted some advice on the case. At the time, neither man knew that the Okazaki and Yu murders were committed by a man named Richard Ramirez. They had no idea that this was just the beginning of Ramirez's killing spree.

> "Frank was the absolute best we had, and I wanted to know what he thought.... He knew serial killers. You couldn't find a better homicide detective anywhere than Salerno."[4]
>
> —Detective Gil Carrillo on Sergeant Frank Salerno

FORENSIC BALLISTICS

When a person fires a gun, the gun leaves microscopic marks on the bullet and cartridge case. Like fingerprints, these marks are unique. When investigators have a suspect's gun, they can fire a test bullet from it. Then they can compare the markings on the test bullet with the markings on any bullets found at the crime scene. An examiner can study the markings to determine if it is likely the bullets were fired from the same gun or if different guns were used.

CHAPTER 2

A VIOLENT HOME

Ricardo "Richard" Ramirez was born in February 1960 in El Paso, Texas. Known as Richie to his family, Richard was the youngest of five children in a Mexican Catholic family. His father, Julian Ramirez, worked for the Santa Fe Railway. His mother, Mercedes, worked at a local boot factory. Neighbors remember that the Ramirez parents were strict and often took their children to church.

Julian had a terrible temper. When Richard's older brothers brought home bad report cards from school or got caught stealing, their father beat them. Once, Julian

Richard Ramirez had a violent and traumatic childhood.

got so mad while installing a kitchen sink that he hit himself in the head with a hammer until he bled. At least one time, Richard was knocked unconscious after being hit by his father. As a result, he often hid until his father's rage had dwindled.

In fifth grade, Richard had a seizure at school. His mother took him to the hospital, where doctors diagnosed him with epilepsy. They explained that Richard was experiencing seizures but told Mercedes there was nothing to worry about. They sent him home without medication or a follow-up appointment.

> "He was pretty much to himself all of the time. There were only four of us of the same age in the neighborhood and he really didn't socialize with any of us."[1]
>
> –Alma Orozco, childhood neighbor of Richard Ramirez

At home, Richard continued to have seizures, but he was never treated for them. In his teens, Richard's seizures occurred less frequently. Eventually, they stopped entirely.

Cousin Mike

When Richard was about 12 years old, his cousin Miguel "Mike" Ramirez returned from the Vietnam War (1954–1975). Like Julian, Mike had a violent temper.

In Vietnam, he could indulge his violent urges and kill without getting in trouble. Mike enjoyed being a soldier.

When Mike returned home to the United States, Richard began to hang out with him. To Richard, Mike was a war hero who had many exciting stories. Mike often bragged about killing many people and assaulting women while he was in Vietnam. Mike even showed Richard photos of himself holding the cut-off head of a woman he had assaulted.

Mike took the young Richard under his wing. He taught Richard the tricks he had learned in the Vietnam jungle. He showed his young cousin how to fight and kill with stealth.

In May 1973, Mike's temper and violent behavior led to a tragedy that Richard witnessed. One day when Mike's wife, Jessie, got home from the grocery store, she complained to Mike that they did not have enough money. Mike told his

TEMPORAL LOBE EPILEPSY

Richard experienced seizures as a child and teen. Some brain experts suggest that he suffered from temporal lobe epilepsy. This is a common form of epilepsy that usually begins between ages ten and 20. Often the person has experienced an injury to the brain or a severe fever in their early life. Seizures involve unusual electrical activity in one or both of the brain's temporal lobes. In some people, temporal lobe epilepsy can cause behavior changes, including changes in sexual behavior and increased aggressiveness.

Richard's cousin Mike may have influenced Richard's later behavior with his stories about violent acts during the Vietnam War.

wife to shut up, but she kept arguing. In response, Mike pulled out a gun. With Richard watching, Mike fatally shot his wife in the face at close range. Eventually, Mike was found not guilty by reason of insanity and sentenced to the Texas State Mental Hospital.

Peeping in Windows

As Richard grew older, he and his father increasingly clashed. The young teen often slept in a nearby cemetery to avoid Julian's anger. At age 13, he moved into his older sister Ruth's home. Ruth had married a young man named Roberto Avala. Avala snuck around the neighborhood at night and peeked into people's windows, hoping to catch a glimpse of naked women or people having sex.

Without Ruth's knowledge, Avala invited Richard to tag along on his nightly expeditions. For Richard, sneaking around in the dark and spying on neighbors was very exciting. Eventually, Ruth found out about their nightly activity and insisted they stop. She and Avala separated.

But even without Avala, Richard continued to sneak out and spy on women. "My brother never slept," Ruth later said. "He was up all night all the time. He was one of those people who functioned with only a few hours of sleep. He'd watch television, or he'd go out somewhere. He just never slept."[2]

Petty Theft

By the time he was a teenager, Richard had established a reputation as a thief. Frances Yvonne Bustillos, who lived a few houses down from the Ramirez family in El Paso, said he was sometimes called "Ricky Robon," meaning "Ricky the Thief" in Spanish. She remembers Richard trying to get into houses in the neighborhood. "I guess at that time, it was more that he was seeing if he could get into the house. At school, he would pick purses and pockets and see how much money he could get. Among his friends, he'd practice," she said.[3]

In 1974, Richard was a freshman at Jefferson High School. He had been an average student during elementary school, but now he skipped classes frequently, and his grades dropped. Richard missed so much school he never progressed past the ninth grade. At age 17, he dropped out of high school entirely.

As a teen in the mid-1970s, Richard began breaking into homes, just as he would do during his killings a decade later.

Drugs, Satan, and Sugar

Around age ten, Richard had begun smoking marijuana, which was cheap and easy to find in El Paso. As a teen, he regularly got high. In addition to marijuana, Richard experimented with other drugs. He tried hallucinogenic drugs such as acid, psilocybin, and peyote. Hallucinogens alter a person's perceptions of the real world and can also affect their thoughts and feelings.

In El Paso, Richard's drug use led to several arrests for marijuana possession and petty theft. As a teen, he also became fascinated with Satan. At night, he would get high, go into the desert, and imagine that he could talk to Satan.

Along with drugs, Richard developed a fondness for junk food. A diet high in sugar combined with poor oral hygiene led to dental problems. His teeth started to rot, which caused his breath to turn foul. "All he would ever eat were chocolates and Pepsi. He'd never brush his teeth. I used to tell him to close

> ## SATANISM
> As a teen, Richard became interested in Satanism. Satanism is a set of beliefs based on Satan, a figure in Christian religious beliefs. Satan, also known as the Devil or Lucifer, is a fallen angel who tempts humans into sin. Often, Satanism involves the worship of Satan. Some modern Satanists believe in Satan as an entity that exists, while others view Satan as a symbol of values they wish to follow.

his mouth or brush his teeth," remembered classmate Ray Garcia.[4]

Attempted Assault

As a teenager, Richard got a job at a local Holiday Inn. He carried luggage, cleaned rooms, and performed maintenance tasks. Richard also peeped in windows to spy on guests and fantasize about the women. Using a master key, he let himself into rooms and stole valuables while the guests slept. He was careful not to get caught.

Richard soon became unsatisfied with simply watching female guests through the windows. He fantasized about going into one of the rooms and assaulting a woman. One night, he broke into a room and attacked a woman. Her husband returned to the room and stopped the assault. Richard was charged as a juvenile, but the charges were dropped when the couple refused to testify.

Move to Los Angeles

By 1978, Richard had grown tired of El Paso. Without telling his family, he boarded a bus for Los Angeles. He listened to heavy metal music through earphones during the ride and slept. In Los Angeles, Richard sold marijuana to make money. He also began using cocaine, first snorting it and then injecting it intravenously. He spent up to $1,500 weekly to buy the drug, so he turned to burglary.[5] He stole anything he could sell quickly, such as televisions, stereos, jewelry, watches, gold, and diamonds.

For a few years, Richard drifted between Los Angeles and San Francisco, California. Earl Gregg Jr. lived with him for a few months during the summer of 1980 in the San Francisco area. Even though they were friends, Gregg felt uneasy about Richard. According to Gregg, he noticed a change in Richard after he started injecting cocaine and became more involved in Satanism. "There's something about him . . . if I had a thousand dollars sitting there, I wouldn't leave the guy alone with it," Gregg said.[6] He noted Richard had become fascinated with guns and knives.

HEAVY METAL MUSIC

Richard was a fan of heavy metal music. He listened to bands such as AC/DC, Metallica, and Judas Priest. In particular, he appeared drawn to the satanic themes in AC/DC's 1979 album, *Highway to Hell*. Richard dropped an AC/DC hat at a crime scene in 1985. He also scrawled the words "Jack the Knife" from Judas Priest lyrics on the wall of another crime scene.[7]

CHAPTER 3

ESCALATING VIOLENCE

On March 28, 1985, 31-year-old pizza parlor manager Bruno Polo drove to Whittier, California. Every night, he dropped off the business's daily receipts at the home of his boss, restaurant owner Vincent Zazzara. When Polo arrived at the home Zazzara shared with his wife, Maxine, he found the front door slightly open. He rang the doorbell, but when no one answered, he pushed the receipts through the mail slot and left.

The following morning, Polo drove back to the Zazzara house. He found the door still ajar in the same position. Polo became suspicious that something was wrong. He rang the doorbell and called for Zazzara, but there was still no answer. Slowly, he opened the screen door and stepped inside the house. Inside, he found Vincent Zazzara's body on the den couch. Bruno ran to a neighbor's house and called Zazzara's son, Peter. Peter called the police.

In early 1985, police began to piece together evidence from multiple crime scenes to conclude that a serial killer was responsible.

Homicide detectives Russ Uloth and J. D. Smith arrived at the Zazzara home around noon. They entered the house, noting that it appeared to have been ransacked. In the den, they found Vincent Zazzara's body. He had been shot in the head. In the bedroom, the detectives discovered Maxine Zazzara's body. Maxine had been shot and stabbed multiple times, and her eyes had been removed.

Detectives Uloth and Smith searched outside the home and found several shoe prints in the flowerbed underneath a window. They noticed marks on the window and frame, as if someone had pried it open. Technicians from the sheriff's crime lab took photos of the bodies, the ransacked house, and the shoe prints. They also made plaster casts of the shoe prints under the window. Analysis of the shoe prints revealed they were made by someone wearing size 11.5 Avia sneakers.

The next day, Dr. Terence Allen performed the autopsies of Vincent and Maxine Zazzara. He removed the bullets from their bodies and noted that a .22-caliber gun had fired them. The bullets were the same type as those found at the Okazaki and Yu murders.

When Carrillo learned about this connection, he gathered more details from Uloth and Smith about the Zazzara murders. The more he discovered, the more he began to think there was a link between this crime and the earlier murders. However, Uloth and Smith disagreed.

> ## LA'S BUS TERMINAL
>
> In 1984, the area near the Los Angeles bus terminal was known to be a dangerous place. Thieves and drug dealers roamed the filthy streets, maneuvering around those who slept outside there. Ramirez was a regular in the area. He would buy drugs, rent a cheap hotel room in the city, and get high for days there. Ramirez got money for drugs by breaking into people's homes and stealing anything of value that he could sell or trade for cash. He wasn't worried about being caught. He believed that demons and Satan were protecting him.

Carrillo hoped ballistics would provide a definite link among the crime scenes. However, the bullets recovered from the Zazzaras were too damaged to compare with the ones from the Okazaki and Yu murders. Carrillo explained his theory to detective Salerno that one person had committed all four murders. Salerno said they would have to wait and see. They needed more evidence.

Kidnappings and Assaults

In early 1985, a series of child abductions and sexual assaults hit the Southern California cities of Montebello, Monterey Park, and Pico Rivera. Detectives from these communities met to coordinate their investigations. The police believed the same person was responsible for the kidnappings because the victims gave similar

FRANK SALERNO

Frank Salerno worked as a detective for 32 years in the Los Angeles County Sheriff's Department.[1] Before the Ramirez case, Salerno was the lead detective in another serial killer investigation, the Hillside Strangler case, in the late 1970s. The Strangler kidnapped, raped, and tortured ten women and girls and dumped their bodies in the Los Angeles hills. While police originally believed the Strangler was a single person, Salerno eventually recognized that the Strangler was actually two men, cousins Kenneth Bianchi and Angelo Buono Jr. Salerno led the task force that solved the case and arrested the two men.

descriptions of their attacker. They described the man as tall and light-skinned with stained teeth. Some said the man smelled terrible.

Carrillo attended the meeting and listened to the investigating detectives describe the details of the crimes, including the sexual assaults. He noticed similarities between the children's descriptions of their attacker and Maria Hernandez's description of the killer at her condo. The detectives also described a shoe print in wet cement found near the scene of an attempted abduction of a girl in Los Angeles. The shoe print was very similar to the print found at the Zazzara house.

Something clicked in Carrillo's mind. He had a feeling that one person was responsible for all of these crimes. "It was like this heavy feeling I had in my gut. I was certain it was all the same guy. I just knew it," he said.[2] Carrillo was the youngest detective in the room, and when he announced his theory, the other detectives laughed. They insisted the crimes were not all related.

Convinced he was right, Carrillo went to Salerno and explained his theory that the suspect in their murder cases was also responsible for the recent kidnappings and sexual assaults. At first, Salerno thought it unlikely. Serial killers usually had a pattern in how they picked

Distinctive shoe prints became key pieces of evidence in the search for the killer.

their victims, where they found their victims, or how they killed their victims. But these crimes had no clear pattern, and the victims were men, women, boys, and girls of various ages. Still, Salerno thought Carrillo's theory was persuasive.

Carrillo and Salerno went to Captain Bob Grimm, head of the Los Angeles County Sheriff's Homicide Bureau. They persuaded him to form a small, informal task force to look into the murders, kidnappings, and sexual assaults. Salerno would lead the task force. "It was extremely challenging to get people to believe, and it truly wasn't easy to convince anybody until Salerno said that this was in fact a serial killer," Carrillo recalled. "Once the experienced man said it, then people started believing."[3]

Salerno handpicked several detectives for the task force, including Uloth, Smith, and Carrillo. The detectives started by reading crime summaries from across Los Angeles County. They searched for any crimes that had shared details.

The Doi Murder and Attack

On May 14, 1985, emergency operator Darlene Boese received a call. The man on the other end weakly begged for help. He passed out before he could identify himself. However, the 911 system automatically recorded the call's address. Boese sent police and emergency responders to the Monterey Park address.

JENNIE VINCOW

On June 27, 1984, Ramirez needed some quick cash. He drove to a nearby community and stopped outside of an apartment building. He spotted an open window, pulled off the screen, and silently entered the apartment of 79-year-old Jennie Vincow. He looked around the apartment, unable to find anything of value to steal. He slipped into the bedroom, where he found Vincow asleep. Armed with a hunting knife, Ramirez fatally stabbed the sleeping Vincow and then escaped into the night. More than a year later, police would link the murder to Ramirez by matching a fingerprint he had left on the window screen.

A little after 5:00 a.m., emergency responders arrived at the home of 66-year-old William "Bill" Doi and his 56-year-old wife, Lillian. They found Bill unconscious and covered in blood. He had been shot in the face but was still breathing. Lillian had been beaten and sexually assaulted. They had been robbed. Lillian was able to describe the suspect as a tall man dressed in black with a gun and bad teeth. Less than an hour later, Bill died of his injuries at the hospital.

Monterey Park homicide detective Paul Torres arrived at the Doi house after 6:00 a.m. He spoke with law enforcement at the scene and walked around looking for evidence. He spotted an Avia shoe print on the muddy ground between the street and the sidewalk. Behind the house, Torres noticed another Avia shoe print under the bedroom window. He found more shoe prints on the patio and a window screen on the ground. He asked the crime scene analysts to make plaster casts of the prints.

Around 8:30 a.m., Carrillo received a call at home. The Monterey Park police had called the sheriff's office and asked for him to come to the Doi crime scene. When he arrived, Detective Torres was surprised. The case was under the jurisdiction of the Monterey Park police, not the Los Angeles County Sheriff's Department where

Monterey Park police responded to the crime scene at the Doi house. The city is located just east of downtown Los Angeles.

Carrillo worked. No one had told him Carrillo had been called, and Torres did not want Carrillo's help. Carrillo left without anyone telling him about the Avia shoe print.

More Attacks

Over the next few weeks, there were more reports of break-ins and attacks in the Los Angeles area. On May 29, 84-year-old Mabel "Ma" Bell and 81-year-old Florence "Nettie" Lang were attacked in their Monrovia home. The assailant drew a pentagram, a five-pointed star enclosed in a circle that is sometimes associated with Satanism, on Bell's body and the walls of their bedrooms. Bell eventually died from her injuries.

The next day, a man broke into Carol Kyle's home in Burbank. The man terrorized Kyle and her 11-year-old son. Then he sexually assaulted her and burglarized the home. The assailant then fled the home but left Kyle and her son alive.

A few weeks later, on July 2, 77-year-old Mary Louise Cannon was found dead in her home in Arcadia, California. A neighbor called the police when he noticed a screen pulled off one of her windows and her belongings tossed around. Police found Cannon's body in the back of the house. Her throat had been slit.

Teen Survivor

On July 4, teen Whitney Bennett opened the bedroom window of her Sierra Madre home. She yelled to her father, who was watering the grass, that he had a phone call. Whitney shut the window but forgot to lock it. After midnight, Whitney went to bed. Her parents were already asleep in their bedroom.

In the early hours of July 5, Whitney woke up in the dark bedroom. She had a horrible, splitting headache. There was blood everywhere. Whitney screamed for her parents and tried to get to the hallway. She collapsed on the floor as her father reached her. He was shocked to

FORENSIC SPOTLIGHT
Casting Shoe Prints

When someone steps in soil or another soft surface, they can leave an impression. To collect impression shoe prints, crime scene examiners use a casting technique. Examiners first take high-resolution photos of the shoe print and the surrounding area. They try to capture as much detail as possible. Next, they collect the shoe print by casting it. Casting uses a powdered stone material that is mixed with water. Examiners carefully pour the mixture into the impression. When the mixture dries, it creates a three-dimensional model of the shoe print.

The collected shoe print and a suspect's shoes are sent to the evidence lab. Examiners use the suspect's shoes to make a comparison sample. Examiners can evaluate the comparison sample and collected evidence side by side. Today, investigators can use searchable databases of shoe outsoles to identify the brand and style of the shoe. Once they have a style identified, they can contact the shoe manufacturer for details on a specific shoe.

Making a cast of a shoe print preserves valuable evidence that could otherwise fade or be easily washed away.

find Whitney had been severely beaten by an unknown attacker and had marks on her neck as if she had been choked. The attacker had left the weapon, a tire iron, in Whitney's bedroom. The Bennetts immediately called the police.

> "It was difficult to believe one man was responsible for everything, since no one in criminal history had been documented doing what Richard did."[4]
>
> –Detective Gil Carrillo

As soon as Carrillo learned about the Bennett attack, he called Salerno. Carrillo was convinced their suspect had attacked Whitney Bennett. The detectives drove to Sierra Madre, where they talked to officers and walked the bloody crime scene. The detectives searched outside the Bennett home, hoping to find evidence to link the crime to the others. However, there were no Avia shoe prints outside. And their killer had never used a tire iron in his previous attacks. Despite these differences, Carrillo and Salerno still suspected it was the same person because of the brutality of the attack.

Crime scene technicians scoured the Bennett home for evidence. It appeared the attacker had been wearing gloves, so it was unlikely he had left any usable fingerprints. Then one of the technicians called the detectives into the bedroom. She carefully unfolded a corner of Whitney's comforter. There was a clear print in blood of an Avia sneaker. "When I saw the print, I got goosebumps all over, chills, and a tight feeling in my gut. It was him—no doubt," Carrillo later said.[5]

A New Sketch

The detectives scanned police reports, looking for crimes and clues that could help them find their killer. At this point, they worked off a rough description of a Hispanic man approximately six feet (1.8 m) tall. The suspect had shaggy black hair and bad teeth, and he wore a size 11.5 shoe.

While reviewing reports, the detectives read about the attack on Carol Kyle in late May. Several case details matched their killer, including the attacker's bad odor and how he entered the Kyle home. Salerno sent task force detectives to interview Kyle. She described her attacker and worked with their sketch artist to create a composite drawing of the attacker. The resulting sketch looked very similar to the attacker Maria Hernandez had seen.

Police sketch artists specialize in using incomplete or conflicting witness descriptions to create images that can be used to help catch suspects.

A CITY GRIPPED BY FEAR

In the early morning of July 8, Deputy Linda Arthur called Carrillo. Arthur worked with Carrillo at the Los Angeles County Sheriff's Department. She explained that her neighbor, Sophie Dickman, had been attacked in her Monterey Park home. Arthur suspected the attacker was the killer Carrillo was after. She asked Carrillo to meet her at the crime scene. Details at the scene were similar to the killer's previous attacks, including a ransacked house. But Carrillo was not sure it was the same man. And no shoe prints had been found.

Carrillo had barely returned home when his beeper went off. The sheriff's office wanted him to head back to Monterey Park. A 61-year-old woman named Joyce Nelson had been brutally murdered in her home less than a mile (1.6 km) from Dickman's house. And the investigating officers had discovered an Avia shoe print at the crime scene.

The killer often used handcuffs to immobilize his victims.

Connecting the Crimes

When Carrillo arrived at Nelson's home, the Monterey Park detectives finally acknowledged what Carrillo had suspected for months. A serial killer and rapist was terrorizing the Los Angeles area. Joe Santoro of the Monterey Park Police Department was one of the officers called to the Nelson crime scene. The grandmother had been beaten to death. "When we went out to the Nelson house, we all had a sick feeling that these were

GIL CARRILLO

Detective Gil Carrillo joined the Los Angeles County Sheriff's Department in 1971 after serving three years in the US Army. In the army, Carrillo saw combat duty in the Vietnam War. As a deputy sheriff, Carrillo started the first plainclothes gang unit in East Los Angeles. He worked in this unit for several years before moving into the homicide bureau. In homicide, Carrillo investigated many types of murders, officer-involved shootings, and serial killings. He remained with the Sheriff's Department for 38 years and became the first Latino promoted to the rank of lieutenant detective in the homicide bureau.[2] Carrillo retired in 2009.

not coincidences, there was someone really terrible and bad out there killing and killing and killing," Santoro said.[1]

At the Nelson home, detectives found Avia shoe prints in the flowerbed and front and back patios. Inside, Nelson's body had been badly beaten. The sneaker's distinct waffle print was clearly visible on her face.

A Plea for the Public's Help

Outside the Nelson home, reporters and photographers gathered. Rumors of a serial killer in the Los Angeles area had been circulating for some time, with the individual crimes being reported in the news. But no one from law enforcement had publicly tied them together.

Monterey Park police chief Jon Elder spoke with Los Angeles County sheriff Sherman Block about joining forces to investigate the connected murders and assaults.

On July 11, Elder spoke at a community meeting and asked for the public's help in identifying the killer. "It will take a combination of police and citizen efforts to break the case. Help us. Be our eyes out there," he said.[3]

Department Cooperation

One of the barriers Carrillo and Salerno faced during the investigation was that the crimes had been committed across Los Angeles County in different jurisdictions. Local police departments took the lead on the crimes in their jurisdictions and did not always share information with other departments. To get investigators on the same page, Carrillo recorded a 20-minute video about the crimes the day after Nelson's murder. The video clearly explained the facts they knew so far and reviewed the

A NEAR MISS

One night in early June 1985, Los Angeles sheriff's deputy John Rodriguez went to bed while his wife, Susan, watched the nightly news. He woke to Susan asking if he had opened a window. Knowing the window was painted shut, he doubted what his wife heard. Susan, who was in the living room, insisted that she had heard a window opening. Early the next morning, deputies investigating the attempted break-in called Carrillo. They had found an Avia shoe print underneath a window. The Night Stalker had been there.

killer's methods, a description of him, and evidence tying the crimes together. He sent the video to all Los Angeles County police departments.

Later that same day, the Los Angeles Police Department (LAPD) allowed the sheriff's office to search a car involved in an attempted abduction in northeast Los Angeles. In early June, a man had tried to kidnap a young girl, but she fought back and ran away. A neighbor saw the attempted abduction and called 911 as the man drove away in a stolen Toyota.

Minutes later, the man ran a red light and was pulled over by LAPD officer John Stavros. The suspect fled on foot, leaving the car behind. Before he ran, the suspect drew a pentagram on the dusty car hood. Stavros searched the car and found a wallet with cash and a dentist appointment card. He had the car towed to a police lot but did not call anyone to dust it for fingerprints.

A few days later, Carrillo read the LAPD's report on the attempted abduction. He and Salerno asked the department if they could examine what had been found in the car. They were denied because it was not their jurisdiction. The LAPD is the primary law enforcement agency for the city of Los Angeles, which is located within Los Angeles County. Salerno suggested that the

Inconsistent cooperation from the LAPD created obstacles for the investigators tracking the killer.

car be fingerprinted. Officials at the LAPD assured him it would be done.

Weeks later, the LAPD finally let the detectives from the sheriff's office access the stolen car. However, the car had been stored in an outdoor police parking lot and had never been dusted for fingerprints. Any fingerprints inside the car were burned away as it sat in the hot sun for weeks. However, another piece of evidence caught Carrillo and Salerno's attention: the dentist appointment card. Multiple witnesses had mentioned the killer's bad teeth. The detectives hoped this might be the break they needed to identify the killer.

The detectives visited Dr. Peter Leung and discovered that the suspect, using the fake name Richard Mena, had recently been in the dentist's office for treatment. Leung explained that the suspect had several painful dental abscesses, and the dentist expected he would be back soon for more dental work. The sheriff's office installed an alarm that the staff could use to quickly let them know if Mena returned. He soon came back, but the alarm malfunctioned and the detectives did not come.

The investigators were not sure that Mena was their man. However, his description and behavior at the attempted Los Angeles abduction matched abductions where the Avia shoe prints had been found. "Our biggest clues were his teeth and feet, and that's where we focused our energy," Salerno said later.[4]

A Killer on the Loose

As detectives worked around the clock to identify the serial killer, his vicious attacks continued. On July 20, Judy Arnold called her parents, 66-year-old Lela and 68-year-old Max Kneiding, before church. When she couldn't reach them, Arnold drove to their Glendale, California, home. No one answered the door even though cars were in the driveway. She walked around the back of the house and noticed a ripped window screen. Uneasy, Arnold entered the home and saw that it had been burglarized. Arnold found her parents' bodies in their bedroom. She screamed and ran away to call the police.

That same day in Sun Valley, homicide detectives were called to the home of 32-year-old Chainarong and Somkid Khovananth. Detectives discovered that Chainarong had been fatally shot while his wife, Somkid, had been sexually assaulted. The attacker had also beaten Somkid, tied up the couple's eight-year-old son, and stolen valuables.

Somkid described her attacker as having brown skin, bad teeth, and black curly hair. She said he was about six feet, one inch (1.85 m) tall and 150 pounds (68 kg). She also told detectives that he had forced her to swear on Satan that she was not hiding valuables from him.

The police departments in Sun Valley and Glendale did not contact the sheriff's office about the new murders

TAKING PRECAUTIONS

Detectives working the Night Stalker case took precautions at home. After an attack near their home, Carrillo's wife and children went to stay with a relative. Carrillo slept alone with a gun near his bed. Salerno was also cautious, as his face and name were frequently in the news regarding the case. Salerno had two dogs that barked when strangers came near. He also tied garbage cans to two doors of his house to ensure the dogs would hear even the quietest intruder. Salerno also slept with his gun within reach.

and assaults. On July 21, Carrillo learned about the two new attacks from a contact at the medical examiner's office. He and Salerno were angry that no one from either police department had contacted them. They arranged to meet detectives at both crime scenes.

At the Kneiding home, the attacker had left no shoe prints, but the crime's brutal nature convinced Carrillo and Salerno that their killer was responsible. At the Khovananth home, however, detectives found the telltale Avia shoe print in the backyard and inside the house. Another connection was found on July 22 when ballistics testing revealed that the gun used in the Kneiding attack was the same gun that had killed Okazaki and Yu.

After surviving the killer's attack, Somkid worked with an LAPD sketch artist on a composite of her attacker. The resulting sketch looked much like the earlier sketches produced with Maria Hernandez and Carol Kyle. The LAPD released the sketch to the public, while police across Southern California taped the sketch to the dashboards of their patrol cars.

The Night Stalker

The serial killer and rapist was now front-page news in California. Journalists from around the country traveled

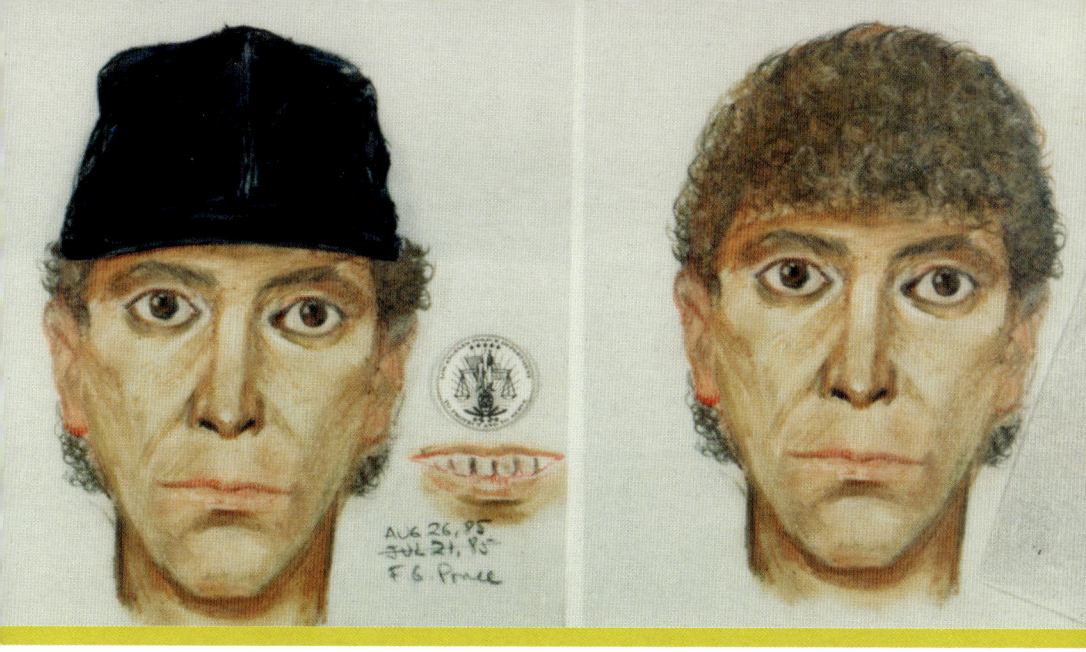

Police sketches of the killer were refined in the summer of 1985 as more witnesses provided details and memories.

to Los Angeles, trying to uncover the details of the killer's crimes. They debated what to call the unidentified serial killer. Some referred to him as the Valley Intruder. Other media outlets called him the Walk-In Killer or the Screen Door Intruder, referencing how he sneaked into his victims' homes. At the *Los Angeles Herald Examiner*, someone suggested the name Night Stalker. The newspaper used the name in print, and it stuck with the public.

Across Southern California, people panicked as they learned about the serial killer on the loose. The Night Stalker's crimes were brutal and random, with victims having little in common. People were terrified they could be the killer's next target. Sales of guns, alarm systems, guard dogs, and window gates skyrocketed. "It's scary. Really scary," said 35-year-old single mother Linda Roberts, who lived north of Los Angeles. "I don't have a gun, but I got a hammer right next to the bed and a baseball bat. And I'm good with a bat."[5]

Glynn Martin was a young officer in the Los Angeles Police Department in 1985. He remembers the fear that swept through Southern California:

> One night, I came home and I was standing in the front of my house. One of my neighbors came up to me to ask what they should do about the killer on the loose, how to stay safe. I told him: lock the windows, lock the door. Then another neighbor came, and another. Soon, there was half a dozen of them, and I was telling them whatever I could. These were people who'd known me since I was five years old. I never thought I'd be standing out in front of that house explaining how to protect themselves from a serial killer.[6]

August Attacks

In early August, the Night Stalker struck again. On August 6, he snuck into the Northridge, California, home of 38-year-old Chris and 27-year-old Virginia Petersen. He shot the husband and wife, but neither was wounded fatally. Chris fought back and chased the Night Stalker out of the house. Both Petersens survived.

Two nights later, on August 8, the Night Stalker broke into the home of Sakina and Elyas Abowath in Diamond Bar, a city in eastern Los Angeles County. He fatally shot Elyas as the man slept. Then the killer handcuffed, beat, and assaulted Sakina. He tied up the couple's three-year-old son and demanded Sakina give him her jewelry. The attacker also insisted that Sakina swear to Satan that she would not look at him. Later analysis of the bullet casings found at the Abowath home showed they matched those from the Petersen home.

> "My boyfriend has got practically everything chained up. We're barricaded in. Last night I couldn't hardly breathe. You get so scared, so scared, you can't sleep."[7]
>
> *—Valerie Peterson, North Hollywood resident, August 1985*

CHAPTER 5

ATTACKS IN SAN FRANCISCO

Through August 1985, the Night Stalker had been connected to crimes only in Southern California. This changed in mid-August when he traveled north to San Francisco. On August 15, the Night Stalker broke into a home in San Francisco's Marina District. The occupants were not home, so he stole some jewelry and left.

Murder in San Francisco

On August 18, the Night Stalker entered Peter and Barbara Pan's home. The Pans lived in a two-story yellow stucco house in the Lakeside District of San Francisco. The Stalker slipped into the house through an unlocked window.

Upstairs, the Stalker found the Pans asleep in their bedroom. He fatally shot 66-year-old Peter Pan in the head. Then he assaulted 64-year-old Barbara and shot her in the head. Leaving Barbara for dead, the Stalker ransacked the house and stole jewelry, watches,

The Night Stalker's move to San Francisco spread terror to Northern California.

and electronics. He grabbed lipstick and wrote a message on the Pans' bedroom wall: "Jack the Knife."[1] He also drew a pentagram. Then he left.

The following day, David Pan stopped by his parents' home for a visit. When he entered the home, Pan found his father murdered and his mother badly wounded. He called the police.

In Southern California, a Glendale detective heard radio chatter about the San Francisco murder and assault. Immediately recognizing similarities to the crimes in Southern California, the detective alerted Carrillo and Salerno. Salerno called San Francisco homicide detective Carl Klotz and learned more details of the crime, including the burglary entry, bullet to the head, and sexual assault.

PENTAGRAM

One of the Night Stalker's trademark symbols was the pentagram. This shape, a five-pointed star inside a circle, is often associated with the devil. The Night Stalker drew a pentagram at several crime scenes and on the hood of a stolen car. He had a pentagram tattooed on his arm. After his arrest, Ramirez reportedly drew a pentagram in blood on his cell floor.

Klotz also described the writing and pentagram the suspect had left on the bedroom wall.

Salerno and Carrillo suspected the Stalker was responsible for the Pan attack. That afternoon, they flew with two LAPD detectives to San Francisco. The men walked through the Pan crime scene and huddled with San Francisco detectives to discuss the case. The Los Angeles detectives compared the Pan attack with the Stalker's earlier crimes. They shared details about their investigation with the San Francisco police. After making an agreement for the two departments to share any further information, the four Los Angeles detectives returned to Southern California.

Warning the Public

A few days after the Pan attack, the San Francisco Police Department issued a statement. It said the department believed there was a link between the Pan murder and the killer terrorizing Los Angeles communities. The police increased patrols in certain areas of the city.

In Los Angeles, Sergeant John Broussard of the Sheriff's Information Bureau acknowledged the potential connection between the cases. However, he declined to provide more details about the evidence found in San Francisco that linked the cases because the investigation was ongoing. He warned that residents in Southern California should remain alert until the Night Stalker was caught. The killer could return to Southern California at any time. "He is extremely diversified, cunning, and very dangerous," Broussard said. "We're still telling people [here] to lock up and light up. We don't want to give a false sense of security."[2]

> "Most serial murderers don't stop. They might relocate. They will kill again."[3]
>
> –Detective Frank Salerno

Clues to the Night Stalker

In their investigation, detectives had noted trademarks and pieces of evidence that appeared across multiple Night Stalker crimes. In many attacks, the Night Stalker entered the home at night, often through an unlocked door or window. Once inside, he quickly killed any adult males with a gunshot to the head. Then he burglarized the homes and assaulted the women. He often used a knife to stab and slash victims in the throat and body. Survivors reported similar wording he used when demanding valuables. Several survivors reported that he made them swear on Satan. At multiple crime scenes, he restrained his victims with handcuffs or thumb cuffs. And he had left a distinctive Avia shoe print at many of the crime scenes.

Carrillo, Salerno, and other detectives working on the investigation purposely did not reveal this critical information to the public. These clues linked the cases to each other and a single suspect. They did not want to let the killer know what information they had on him.

A Disastrous Press Conference

On August 23, San Francisco mayor Dianne Feinstein held a press conference at City Hall about the Night Stalker. "This is a very serious situation. The killer goes into a

SERIAL KILLER TRADEMARKS

Serial killers often leave trademark clues at their crime scenes, according to Harvey Schlossberg, a forensic psychologist who worked on the Son of Sam murders in New York City in 1976 and 1977. "Each killing is a lot like an artist's painting, based on the artist's needs and wishes, so there has to be some sort of element that ties them together," said Schlossberg. "In these serial murders, you have the same dynamic. Each one has the same touch that will distinguish it from anyone else's."[4]

Dianne Feinstein was mayor of San Francisco from 1978 to 1988, and she later became a US senator.

home at night and kills . . . at random," she said. Feinstein stressed the importance of the public being vigilant and reporting anything unusual to the police. "Somewhere in the Bay Area, someone is renting a room, an apartment or a home to this vicious serial killer. I am hoping that people will look at this composite drawing," Feinstein said, holding up a composite sketch of the suspect.[5] Feinstein also announced a $10,000 reward for information leading to the arrest and conviction of the killer. The new reward brought the total statewide reward to $35,000.[6]

Then, Feinstein described the evidence that linked the Pan crime scene to other crimes throughout California. She revealed that ballistics had matched the gun used

UNIQUE SNEAKERS

The Avia shoe prints found at multiple Night Stalker crime scenes were from a unique size and style of shoe. At the time, only six pairs of that Avia sneaker model in a size 11.5 had been sold in the United States. Five pairs were sold in Arizona. Only one pair was sold in Los Angeles.[8] Police knew that if they found the owner of the size 11.5 Avia sneaker, it was likely he was their killer.

at the Pan crime scene to the same one used in two of the Los Angeles murders. She also revealed that police had found Avia shoe prints at multiple crime scenes.

Salerno and Carrillo watched Feinstein's press conference on television. They were furious that the mayor had revealed specific details about the investigation that the police had purposely not made public. Now the Night Stalker could avoid leaving the evidence that linked him to multiple crimes. They felt Feinstein's poorly timed comments could put the entire investigation in jeopardy.

When he learned about Feinstein's comments, Los Angeles County sheriff Sherman Block spoke to Salerno and Carrillo. He shared their anger. That evening, Block held a press conference and criticized public officials for recklessly making the details of the investigation public. "It places this community in jeopardy because it impedes our ability to go forward fully with the investigation," Block said.[7]

Evidence Destroyed

The detectives feared the Night Stalker would destroy evidence after Feinstein's press conference. They were right. He saw the press conference on the news. He did not know he had left Avia shoe prints at different crime scenes, and he did not know that his gun had been connected to multiple murders. Now he did.

Around 8:00 p.m. on the day of the press conference, the Night Stalker walked onto San Francisco's Golden Gate Bridge. As the sun set over the San Francisco Bay, the Stalker dropped his size 11.5 Avia sneakers into the water. The strong water currents in the bay carried the shoes away forever.

Sherman Block served as the Los Angeles County sheriff throughout most of the 1980s and 1990s.

CHAPTER 6

A BREAK IN THE CASE

On August 23, 13-year-old James Romero and his family returned home to Mission Viejo in Southern California after a camping vacation. James was enjoying his summer break, hanging out with friends and a new girlfriend. That morning, the front-page headline of the *Los Angeles Times* announced that a recent murder in San Francisco had been linked to the serial killer terrorizing Southern California. However, James did not watch the news or read newspapers. At the time, he knew nothing about the Night Stalker.

A summer heat wave made it uncomfortably hot that night, and James had trouble sleeping. He entered the garage late at night and began working on his minibike. Then he heard footsteps. "All of a sudden, I hear footsteps in the gravel. Crunch, crunch, crunch, crunch," he remembered.[1] James ran inside and woke up his parents. They called the police. James looked outside and watched

Carns survived the Night Stalker's brutal attack and later moved to North Dakota.

as a tall man dressed in black drove away in an orange Toyota hatchback with a roof rack. James was able to see part of the car's license plate.

At first, the Romeros and the police thought a simple prowler had been walking around their home. Then news broke that there had been another Night Stalker attack nearby. On August 25, 29-year-old Bill Carns and his fiancée, 29-year-old Inez Erickson, were attacked while sleeping in their Mission Viejo home. The Night Stalker shot Carns in the head three times and then assaulted Erickson. He forced Erickson to hand over valuables and

> "He would pick out a particular place to go inside, rather than picking out his victims in advance. He was kind of an opportunist."[3]
>
> –Holly Pera, San Francisco homicide inspector

swear on Satan she had given him everything. He also told her to "tell them the Night Stalker was here."[2]

Orange County homicide detectives called Salerno and Carrillo, who drove to the Carns crime scene. The detectives saw the ransacked house, and they learned details of the attack. They were confident the Night Stalker had returned to Southern California.

Search for an Orange Toyota

Police quickly realized that James had seen the Night Stalker. Every police officer in Southern California was on the lookout for the orange Toyota that the teen had described. Finding the car might be the break they needed to find the killer. Then a tip came in about the car. An orange Toyota that matched the police description had been stolen from Los Angeles's Chinatown earlier. The caller gave police the complete license plate number of the stolen car. It matched the partial number that James had remembered seeing. The sheriff's department released the license plate number to the press.

Law enforcement hoped that someone in the surrounding area might see the car.

On August 28, the orange Toyota was found abandoned in a shopping center in Los Angeles County. At first, the police did not move the car. They watched and waited for a full day and night, hoping the Stalker would return to it. When he did not appear, the police loaded the car onto a flatbed truck and took it to a police garage.

Technicians carefully combed the car for evidence the Stalker might have left behind. They found a clear fingerprint on the outside of the rearview mirror. Technicians dusted the print with black powder and removed it with lifting tape. Now they had a fingerprint they believed belonged to the Stalker. However, detectives needed a suspect to compare it against to make a match.

FINDING AND LIFTING FINGERPRINTS

Fingerprints at a crime scene can link a suspect to the scene. Investigators search for fingerprints by dusting surfaces with a dark powder that sticks to and reveals the prints. When investigators find crime scene fingerprints, they use clear adhesive tape to lift the prints and preserve them for the investigation. While a fingerprint shows that a suspect was at a crime scene, it does not explain why they were there or what they did.

FORENSIC SPOTLIGHT
Fingerprint Analysis

No two people have the same fingerprints. Every person's fingerprints have a unique pattern of loops, whorls, and arches. Fingerprint analysis can be used to identify suspects and place a suspect at the scene of a crime.

When a fingerprint is found at a crime scene, crime scene technicians lift it and send it to the evidence lab for evaluation. At the lab, fingerprint examiners first determine if the print is good enough to be used. Next, the examiner will compare the crime scene print and a known print side by side. A known print is one collected from a suspect, victim, or other person present at the scene.

The examiner compares the characteristics of the two prints to determine if they match. They use a small magnifier called a loupe to see the tiniest characteristics, called minutiae, of the fingerprint. If enough details are the same, the fingerprints likely come from the same person.

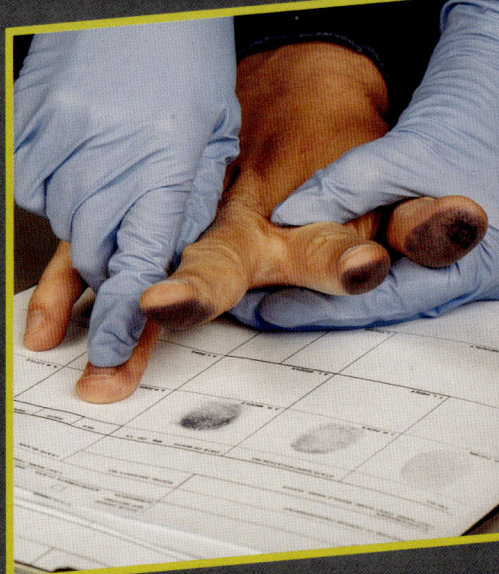

Even identical twins have unique sets of fingerprints.

Today, investigators use computer systems to aid in this work. They can quickly search local, state, and national fingerprint databases for possible matches. Fingerprint examiners review the possible matches and decide if the prints are from the same source.

A Man Named Rick

On August 27, another tip came in to the sheriff's task force. A woman called to tell detectives that her father, Jesse Perez, knew the Night Stalker's identity. She explained that Perez had met a man named Rick from Texas near the Los Angeles bus terminal. Rick had bad teeth, talked about Satan, and claimed to be a talented burglar. The woman explained that her father hesitated to talk to the police because he was frightened.

When detectives met with Perez and his daughter, Perez nervously told them about Rick. He did not know Rick's last name but believed he had come to California from El Paso. Perez told detectives he bought a .22-caliber gun from Rick, just like the one that had been used in several of the Night Stalker's murders. However, Perez no longer possessed the gun, as he had given it to a friend in Mexico for protection. Perez also told detectives about Felipe Solano, a man Rick met with to buy and sell stolen goods.

GUN FOUND IN MEXICO

In September 1985, detectives from the Los Angeles County Sheriff's Department recovered the gun that Jesse Perez said he got from his friend Rick. They found it in Tijuana, Mexico. Police believe that Ramirez used the gun in some of his crimes. The weapon was a .22-caliber semiautomatic pistol. Forensic testing later confirmed that the gun had been used to kill William Doi in Monterey Park.

At Solano's house, detectives hit the jackpot. They found many items that had been stolen in the Stalker's robberies. They questioned Solano about Rick, but Solano swore he did not know the man's last name or how to contact him. He said that Rick contacted him only when he had something to sell.

Leads in San Francisco

Meanwhile, in San Francisco, the task force working on the case pursued a different angle. Detectives published photos and descriptions of the jewelry stolen from Peter and Barbara Pan. They hoped someone would recognize the jewelry and call in a tip to help them identify the Night Stalker.

The break police needed came from Donna Meyers of Lompoc, California. After the police published information about the stolen jewelry, Meyers's daughter and son-in-law recognized one of the bracelets as one that Meyers's friend, Rick, had

ADDING UP THE REWARD

As the Night Stalker terrorized Southern California, several rewards were offered for information leading to the identification, arrest, and conviction of the serial killer. Statewide, about $80,000 was offered by various jurisdictions and the governor's office.[4] Individuals and corporations in California contributed to the rewards in hopes of catching the killer.

given to her. They called the police. Rick was from El Paso and bragged about being a thief. He often talked about Satan and constantly listened to heavy metal music. They described Rick as having stained, chipped teeth. They had also seen that Rick had a gun matching the description of those used in the crimes.

San Francisco homicide detective Frank Falzon questioned Donna Meyers. They pressed her for Rick's last name. Meyers did not know it, but she told them that her friend Armando Rodriguez did. Detectives questioned Rodriguez. At first, he refused to talk to the police. But eventually, he told them that Rick's last name was Ramirez.

Identifying the Night Stalker

The San Francisco detectives searched their computer databases for suspects named Rick, Richard, or Ricardo Ramirez. The search returned thousands of people. Detectives spread out in the city. They interviewed hotel managers and showed them the composite sketch of the suspect. The manager of the Bristol Hotel said a man who matched the Stalker's description had stayed at the hotel. Detectives searched the man's room and found a pentagram drawn on the bathroom door, just like the one found at the Bell and Pan crime scenes.

Computerized fingerprint databases were a major leap forward for police departments in the 1980s.

In Los Angeles, detectives Salerno and Carrillo now had a name to match the fingerprint found in the stolen orange Toyota. Using a computer, they searched through everyone named Ramirez in police files to see if anyone matched the print. One came back as a perfect match.

Richard Muñoz Ramirez from El Paso, Texas, had been arrested in December 1984 for stealing a car. They showed Ramirez's 1984 mug shot to Jesse Perez. Perez confirmed that the man in the photo was the Rick he had described to the police. Finally, the police had a name and a face for the serial killer. Richard Ramirez was the Night Stalker.

CHAPTER 7

CAPTURING THE KILLER

Investigators now knew the identity of the Night Stalker. They debated whether it would be a good idea to share this information with the public. Because Ramirez did not know the police had identified him, the authorities had the element of surprise on their side. If the police released his photo to the public to warn them, it might give Ramirez time to evade capture and escape.

Going Public

Los Angeles County sheriff Sherman Block decided the risk of Ramirez killing again was too great. On August 30, he called a press conference at the Hall of Justice in the Los Angeles Civic Center. Word quickly spread among the press that the police had finally identified a suspect in the string of murders and assaults. Hundreds of reporters gathered to hear the news.

At August 30 press conferences in Los Angeles and San Francisco, authorities revealed the identity of the infamous Night Stalker.

Sheriff Block stood with Los Angeles police chief Daryl Gates and Orange County sheriff Brad Gates before the gathered reporters. He told them that the suspect in the Night Stalker killings and assaults was a man named Richard Ramirez, a 25-year-old from El Paso, Texas. Block described Ramirez as having a criminal background with convictions for drug possession and driving a vehicle without the owner's permission. Block said that Ramirez was considered "armed and dangerous." "We are satisfied that we now know the identification of the individual known as the Night Stalker. . . . All police agencies in California and surrounding states have been notified," said Sheriff Block.[1]

The police released a photo of Ramirez. It had been taken when he was arrested in 1984 in Los Angeles on suspicion of driving a stolen vehicle. Ramirez's photo looked very similar to the composite drawing that police had previously distributed of the suspect in the Night Stalker murders and assaults.

Police described Ramirez as Latino with black hair and brown eyes. He weighed approximately 155 pounds (70 kg) and stood about six feet, one inch (1.85 m) tall. The police also highlighted Ramirez's distinctive decayed teeth. At one point during the press conference, Sheriff Block spoke directly to Ramirez: "You cannot escape. Every law officer and every citizen now knows exactly what you look like and who you are."[2]

By the next day, Ramirez's photo was on the front page of every newspaper in California. News bulletins interrupted television broadcasts across the country to show Ramirez's photo and name him as the suspect in the Night Stalker crimes. Thousands of copies of Ramirez's photo were distributed to law enforcement officers in Los Angeles County. Everyone was looking for him.

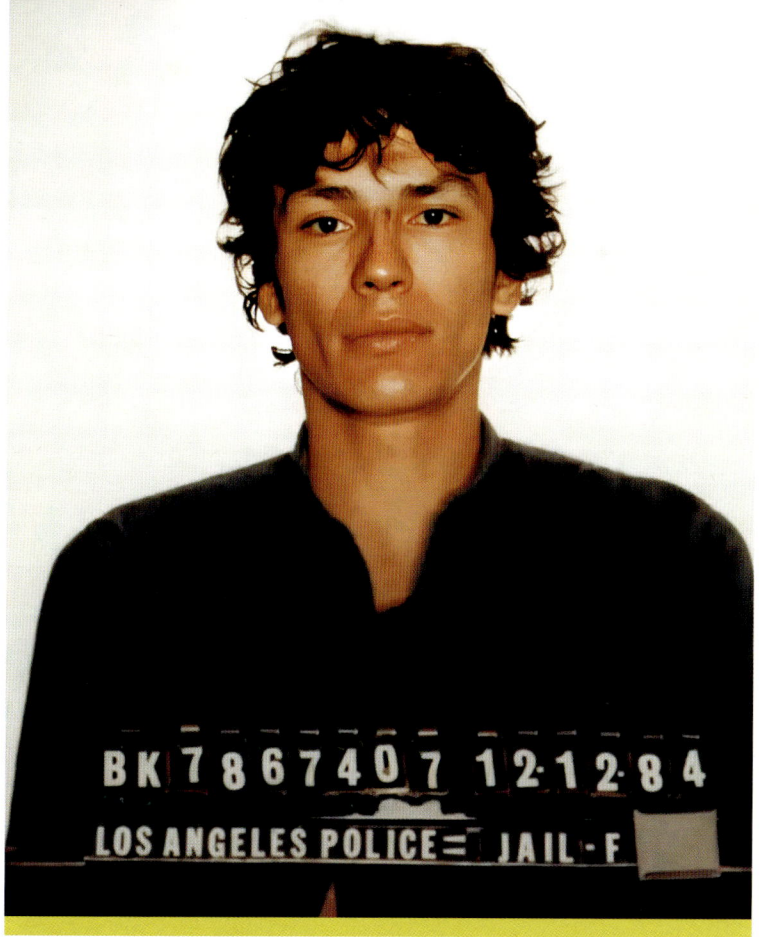

A 1984 mugshot of Ramirez was the public's first glimpse of the killer's face.

Arizona Trip

Hours before the police press conference, Ramirez had boarded a Greyhound bus to Tucson, Arizona. He planned to visit his brother Robert, who lived in Tucson with his wife and daughter. During the bus ride, Ramirez listened to heavy metal music with headphones. He had no idea the police had identified him as the Night Stalker.

When he arrived in Tucson, Ramirez called Robert from the bus station, but his brother was not home.

Ramirez decided to wait at the bus station and try calling later. As he waited, Ramirez noticed an increased police presence at the station. Ramirez did not know that after the Los Angeles police had identified him, they also discovered he had a brother in Tucson. The Los Angeles police alerted the Tucson Police Department to be on the lookout for the dangerous serial killer.

Ramirez felt increasingly uncomfortable near the officers, so he changed his plans and bought a return ticket to Los Angeles. The officers were watching buses arriving from Los Angeles, so they did not notice Ramirez slipping onto a bus headed back to the city. The bus was scheduled to arrive in Los Angeles at 7:45 a.m. on Saturday, August 31. Ramirez slid into a window seat, closed his eyes, and fell asleep.

Return to Los Angeles

Ramirez woke as the bus arrived in Los Angeles. About 15 LAPD Special Investigation Section (SIS) officers were stationed around the bus terminal. They suspected Ramirez might try to escape Los Angeles via bus, so they focused on the outgoing buses and passengers. Ramirez was able to exit his bus and walk through the terminal without being spotted.

Outside, the summer heat was stifling. Ramirez walked to a nearby store to buy a coffee and a pastry. He noticed a few older women in the store pointing at him as he paid. He heard one of them call him "the Killer" in Spanish.[3] Then Ramirez glanced at the store's newspaper rack. His picture was plastered on the front page of every edition. He grabbed a copy of one paper and quickly left the store.

The Chase Begins

The store clerk recognized Ramirez from his picture in the news and called the police. Within minutes, sirens

Despite police surveillance, Ramirez managed to evade capture at the bus terminal.

blared as every officer in East Los Angeles headed toward the area looking for Ramirez. Police helicopters flew overhead, searching for the man they believed to be the Night Stalker.

Ramirez ran. He sprinted toward the Santa Ana Freeway, leaving his black backpack behind. He hopped a fence and ran down a tree-covered hill toward the freeway. Cars sped by on the freeway, and Ramirez waited for a break in the traffic to dash across the busy roadway. He reached a bus stop, boarded a bus heading south, and sat down.

However, the bus passengers recognized Ramirez immediately from his picture on television and in newspapers. They began to point at him. When Ramirez realized everyone knew his face, he got off the bus at its next stop. He was desperate to find a place to hide. It was too risky to take public transportation. He needed a car.

Manuela Villanueva and her boyfriend, Carmello Robles, parked their car at a grocery store a little after 8:00 a.m. Robles entered the store while Villanueva waited in the car. Ramirez ran up to the car and demanded Villanueva get out. When she refused, he grabbed her arm and tried to pull her out of the car. As Villanueva screamed for help, Robles ran from the store. Arthur Benavedes, who

Police helicopters joined the hunt as the authorities closed in on Ramirez.

owned a nearby barbershop, also ran out to see what was causing the commotion. He was shocked to recognize the face of the Night Stalker, whom he had just seen in the morning newspaper.

Ramirez ran again and ducked down an alley while Robles chased him. Frank Moreno was exiting a building in the alley, saw the chaos, and joined Robles in the chase. Ramirez hopped over another fence and ran through several backyards. He kept moving toward Hubbard Street.

Captured by Angry Residents

Hubbard Street was in a part of town where many Mexican Americans lived. Local residents knew that Ramirez had been identified as the Night Stalker. The fact that Ramirez was Mexican had caused a significant stir in East Los Angeles's Mexican American community. Everyone was talking about him.

Ramirez ran into the backyard of Luis Munoz, who was cooking on his barbecue grill. Munoz demanded to know why Ramirez was running through his yard. When Ramirez did not answer, Munoz struck him with his barbecue spatula.

Ramirez kept running and jumped over a fence into Faustino Pinon's backyard. That morning, Pinon had been working on his daughter's red sports car. He had left the car running while he stepped inside to grab a tool. Ramirez jumped into the car, but Pinon emerged from the house and stopped him before he could drive away.

Ramirez got out of the car and ran across the street. Twenty-eight-year-old Angelina De La Torre had just parked her car in front of her house. As De La Torre exited her car, Ramirez rushed toward her. She recognized him immediately from the news and began to scream. Ramirez demanded that Angelina give him her keys. When she resisted, he punched her in the stomach and ripped the keys from her hand.

Manuel De La Torre heard his wife's screams and ran to her. He grabbed a long metal rod he used to close the front gate. As Ramirez tried to start the car, Manuel hit him on the head with the metal rod. Ramirez jumped out of the car and began running down Hubbard Street.

Manuel and a few neighbors chased him down the street. "I ran behind him, and I hit him harder over the head with the metal bar, and that's when he went down," said Manuel.[4] The commotion drew more people out of their homes. Some of them had armed themselves with bats and clubs.

The men surrounded Ramirez. He was on the ground, and blood was running down the side of his head. Marina Vargas lived on Hubbard Street, and she went outside to see what was happening. She saw several of her neighbors surrounding a man sitting on the sidewalk. "They had him trapped and were waiting for the police to arrive. A neighbor had the newspaper and said that it was the murderer who the police sought," said Vargas.[5]

> "Catching him is one thing. Now the real detective work starts, trying to piece together all these cases."[6]
>
> –Frank Falzon, San Francisco homicide inspector

Police Arrive

Sheriff's Deputy Andres Ramirez was the first officer to arrive at the scene, responding to a report of a man with a gun. When he arrived, he saw a crowd gathered around a man bleeding on the sidewalk. He looked at the man and recognized him as the Night Stalker. Ramirez reportedly told him in Spanish, "I'm lucky the police got here. It's me. It's me. It's me."[7] Deputy Ramirez arrested Richard Ramirez and handcuffed him.

More police arrived at the scene within minutes. Unsure if they had the right suspect in custody, police ordered Ramirez to open his mouth so they could look at his teeth. Now convinced he was their man, police drove Ramirez to the Los Angeles Police Department's Hollenbeck station. Detectives Carrillo and Salerno met Ramirez at the station. "It was a great feeling—we'd been

LINEUP

A few days after his arrest, police placed Ramirez in a police lineup. About 30 surviving victims, relatives, and witnesses came to the jail to see if they could pick the suspect out of the lineup. Ramirez wore number 2 in the lineup. Each man in the lineup was asked to read statements the Night Stalker had allegedly said. One of the witnesses was six-year-old Anastasia Hronas, who was kidnapped and assaulted by the Night Stalker. When Detective Carrillo asked if the witnesses had any questions, the young girl was certain who it was, simply asking if she should "write the word two or the number 2."[8]

Police took Ramirez into custody on August 31, just one day after his identity became public knowledge.

chasing, up until the night before, an unknown person and now he was in custody," said Carrillo.⁹

Word of Ramirez's arrest spread quickly. Crowds gathered outside the police station, hoping to catch a glimpse of the killer. Around 3:30 p.m., Ramirez was brought out of the station's back door and put into a police car between two officers. As Ramirez was driven away to the Central Jail, the crowd erupted into loud cheers. One teenage boy had waited two hours to see the infamous Night Stalker. "He sure doesn't look mean. He just looks every day, doesn't he?" the boy said.¹⁰

CHAPTER 8

TRIAL AND CONVICTION

After his arrest, Ramirez was charged with 15 murders—14 in Los Angeles County and one in San Francisco. He was also initially charged with more than 50 additional felonies, including attempted murder, sexual assault, burglary, robbery, and kidnapping.[1] Los Angeles deputy district attorney Phil Halpin asked for Ramirez to be held without bail because of the seriousness of the crimes. The judge agreed.

Preparing for Trial

At first, Ramirez was assigned two public defenders. However, the Ramirez family hired defense lawyers Daniel Hernandez and Arturo Hernandez, who are not related, to represent him. The lawyers had no experience in death penalty cases, and the judge was concerned that they would not be able to handle the complex trial. However, Ramirez insisted that he wanted them. He arranged to

Ramirez was represented in court by defense attorneys Daniel Hernandez, *left*, and Arturo Hernandez, *right*.

pay them by assigning them any movie or book rights about his life. Eventually, the judge allowed them to take Ramirez's case.

In October 1985, Ramirez was led into a crowded courtroom for arraignment wearing manacles and leg irons. His new attorneys entered a plea of not guilty to all charges. Before leaving the courtroom, Ramirez flashed the palm of his hand to people in the courtroom. On his palm, Ramirez had drawn a pentagram. As officers led him from the courtroom, Ramirez shouted, "Hail Satan!"[2]

After nearly three years of pretrial motions and delays, jury selection began in July 1988. The selection process took nearly six months to finish. During that time, Judge Michael Tynan, prosecutors, and defense attorneys questioned about 1,600 potential jurors.[3] Anyone selected would need to be available for what was expected to be a lengthy trial. Twelve jurors and 12 alternate jurors were selected.[4]

EXTRA COURTROOM SECURITY

In 1988, a jail employee reported to officials that he had overheard Ramirez threatening to shoot and kill the prosecutor in his case. Ramirez claimed that someone in the courtroom would pass him a gun to use. He reportedly planned to open fire on others in the courtroom as well. After Judge Tynan was made aware of the threat, a metal detector was installed in the hallway outside the courtroom. Ramirez remained in leg shackles when he appeared in court during the trial.

The Prosecution's Case

The Ramirez trial began in January 1989. One of the initial 14 murder charges in Los Angeles County had been dropped, as the prosecution did not have the physical evidence needed to tie the case to the other murders. Several felony charges had also been dropped as witnesses had died or the parents of young children refused to let them testify in court. Now, Ramirez faced 43 charges, including 13 counts of murder, five attempted murders, 11 sexual assaults, and 14 burglaries.[5]

Deputy District Attorney Halpin, the lead prosecutor in the trial, gave a two-hour opening statement. Halpin outlined the case against Ramirez, systematically detailing the 13 murders Ramirez was charged with committing. He pointed to a large map of Los Angeles County marked with the locations of the crimes and a chart of the murders and sexual assaults. Halpin told the jury that the prosecution would present evidence such as fingerprints, ballistics tests, and eyewitness testimony. He asked for the death penalty.

Over the next three months, the prosecution, led by Halpin and Alan Yochelson, presented its massive case against Ramirez. It called 137 witnesses to testify and presented 521 exhibits and pieces of evidence linking Ramirez to the crimes. Eight eyewitnesses identified Ramirez as their attacker or placed him at a crime scene.[6]

Prosecutors presented evidence of the Avia shoe prints found at seven of the 15 crime scenes. Although the shoes were never recovered, prosecutors linked them to

ANOTHER VICTIM?

Ramirez was initially charged with the murder of Patty Higgins, a 32-year-old teacher. On June 27, 1985, Higgins was found dead in her Arcadia apartment. Her throat had been slashed. However, prosecutors decided to drop this murder charge from the trial as they believed they did not have enough evidence to confidently link the Higgins murder to Ramirez.

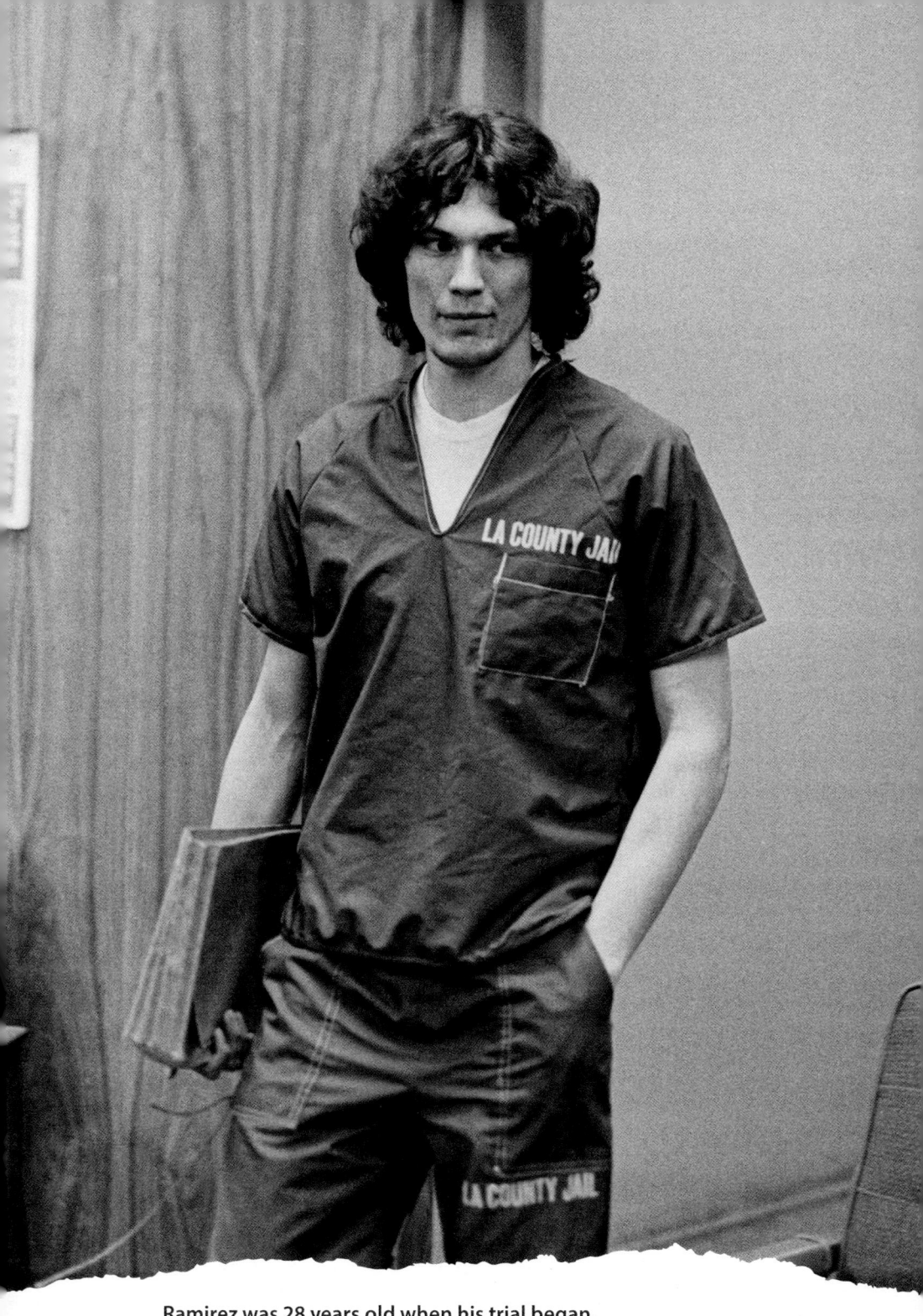
Ramirez was 28 years old when his trial began.

Ramirez by presenting evidence from a burglary in May 1985, where police found both a shoe print and a palm print. Prosecutors presented about 375 pieces of jewelry and other property stolen from seven crime scenes that were found and linked to Ramirez.[7]

Four different guns were used in the Night Stalker crimes, but only one was found. However, prosecutors presented evidence linking the gun that killed the Zazzaras to the same one used to murder Chainarong Khovananth. Prosecutors also presented evidence found in a suitcase Ramirez kept at the Los Angeles bus terminal. The suitcase contained many items with Ramirez's fingerprints, including unused ammunition for the types of guns used in several Night Stalker murders.

> "The memory of what happened never leaves; it's ingrained as a part of your life, just like the color of your hair."[8]
>
> –Virginia Petersen, a victim of Richard Ramirez

Prosecutors emphasized the similarities in how Ramirez committed the crimes. At several crime scenes, they said, Ramirez wore gloves, used similar language when talking with his victims, used blunt objects to beat his victims, and used similar restraints to tie up his victims. In about half of the crime scenes, he allegedly sneaked into the victim's home through an unlocked door or window.

The Defense's Case

The defense was led by attorneys Daniel Hernandez, Arturo Hernandez, and Ray Clark, whom the judge had appointed in March 1989 to help with the case. At first, Ramirez believed the prosecution had not proven its case against him and did not want to present a defense. However, his lawyers convinced him that allowing them to present a defense in court was in his best interest.

The defense's strategy was to show the jury that the prosecution's evidence was inconsistent or defective. It presented evidence of unidentified fingerprints, blood, and hairs found at several crime scenes that did not belong to Ramirez or his alleged victims. Ramirez's father, Julian, testified that his son was in El Paso, Texas, visiting family at the time of two of the alleged attacks. The alibi was later challenged by a prosecution witness, a dentist who said he treated Ramirez in Los Angeles on one of the dates in question.

The defense also attempted to cast doubt on the accuracy of eyewitness testimony in the case. It argued that many of the witnesses' initial descriptions of their

Ramirez spoke with his attorneys just before they began presenting their case in May 1989.

attacker were inaccurate and inconsistent. Some of the initial descriptions included different hair colors and races. Some eyewitnesses were inconsistent in how they described the attacker's teeth. The defense also argued that witnesses had identified Ramirez in a police lineup only after they had seen his picture in newspapers and on television.

Psychologist Elizabeth Loftus was brought in to testify. She was an expert in memory and eyewitness identifications from the University of Washington. She explained that the stress of the attacks could have affected the eyewitnesses' ability to remember details accurately.

The defense presented Ramirez as a nonviolent petty thief throughout their case. "It's obvious we believe he's not responsible for the crimes," said Daniel Hernandez

PSYCHOLOGICAL PROFILE

Mental health experts who examined Ramirez for trial presented a disturbing profile of the man. They suggested his troubled childhood and exposure to violence contributed to his later crimes. After his arrest, Ramirez showed no remorse for his crimes and appeared to enjoy the suffering he had caused his victims. Experts concluded that he suffered from several psychological disorders, such as antisocial personality disorder and substance use disorders.

to reporters. Clark added, "We're trying to raise reasonable doubt (in the jurors' minds). We're trying to show the weaknesses in the prosecution's case."[9]

As it closed its case, the defense showed the jury a picture of Ramirez as a family man. The photo showed Ramirez with his parents and niece. Ramirez's sister-in-law testified that the picture was taken at the Ramirez family home by the defendant's sister, Rosa Flores. It was taken on May 25, 1985, to celebrate Ramirez's niece's first communion.

Closing Arguments

In July 1989, the prosecution and defense presented their closing arguments. Each side highlighted the strengths of its case and the weaknesses of the other side's case. Prosecutor Halpin urged the jury to convict Ramirez of the gruesome crimes that he called "acts of cowardice."[10]

Defense lawyer Clark told the jury that the prosecution had not proven its case beyond a reasonable doubt. He argued that witnesses had wrongly identified his client as the Night Stalker. "I'm asking you to go in, take a look at all the evidence, discuss it among yourselves and come back with 43 not-guilty verdicts," Clark said to the members of the jury.[11]

Deliberation and Verdict

In late July, the jury began its deliberations. One juror kept falling asleep during deliberations and was replaced with an alternate. On August 14, juror Phyllis Singletary did not arrive for deliberations. When officers went to her home, they discovered that she had been shot to death, a victim of a domestic dispute unrelated to the trial. The judge replaced Singletary with an alternate juror, and deliberations continued.

On September 20, 1989, the jury of seven women and five men returned with their verdict after 22 days of deliberations.[12] Before the verdicts were read, Ramirez was allowed to leave the packed courtroom. He listened to the verdicts through a speaker in a holding cell in the courthouse. The jury found Ramirez guilty on all charges.

On October 4, the same jury recommended that Ramirez be sentenced to death. On November 7, Ramirez appeared in court for formal sentencing. Before sentencing, Ramirez spoke to the courtroom, saying, "You don't understand me. I am beyond good and evil. I will be avenged. Lucifer dwells in us all."[13]

> **"Big deal. Death always went with the territory. See you in Disneyland."[14]**
>
> –Richard Ramirez to reporters after being sentenced to death

Judge Tynan denied a defense motion to reduce Ramirez's sentence to life in prison without parole. As he formally announced Ramirez's death sentence, Tynan said, "Richard Ramirez terrorized the people of this county for over a year during his senseless and brutal murder spree. The existence of the death penalty was not a deterrent to Richard Ramirez. The jury has found that death is a just and fitting penalty for his crimes."[15]

ADDITIONAL CHARGES

In December 1985, Ramirez was charged in Orange County for the attack in Mission Viejo on Bill Carns and Inez Erickson. Prosecutors charged Ramirez with eight felonies, including attempted murder and rape.[16] However, when Ramirez was found guilty and sentenced to death in the Los Angeles trial, Orange County prosecutors announced they would not move forward with the case in their jurisdiction, sparing the victims from having to testify in court.

CHAPTER 9

LIFE AND DEATH BEHIND BARS

After sentencing, Ramirez was transferred to California's San Quentin State Prison. San Quentin is located in Marin County, about a 30-minute drive from San Francisco. In California at the time, all men sentenced to death were sent to San Quentin.

Security Risk

California law enforcement saw Ramirez as a security risk. Many female admirers and Satanists had attended his trial, and rumors swirled about plans to break him out of prison. Therefore, officials decided flying him

San Quentin is a large, secure prison that has held many notorious serial killers.

to San Quentin would be safer than driving. A helicopter landed on the roof of the Los Angeles County jail to pick up Ramirez and three guards. Ramirez was shackled at the wrists and ankles.

Initially, Ramirez was taken to San Quentin's Adjustment Center block for evaluation. In this prison block, inmates were restricted to their cells nearly 24 hours a day. He was put in a six-by-eight-foot (1.8 by 2.4 m) cell with a toilet, sink, and bunk bed.[1]

In February 1990, Ramirez was transferred to the San Francisco County jail so that he could be closer to court for the Pan murder and assault charges that he still faced. Lawyers from the San Francisco Public Defender's Office represented him. In the county jail, Ramirez had access to a telephone and television. He could also interact with other prisoners. Soon after his arrival, Ramirez got into a fight with another inmate. He sent a strong message to everyone in the jail that he was

SAN QUENTIN

Opened in 1854, San Quentin State Prison is California's oldest prison. It is a maximum-security prison for men and is well-known for several infamous inmates, including Richard Ramirez and cult leader Charles Manson. In 2019, California governor Gavin Newsom ordered a halt to all state executions and the immediate closure of the execution chamber at San Quentin. At the time, California had 737 inmates on death row.[2]

not someone to mess with. As a result, the other inmates left him alone. Ramirez returned to San Quentin in 1993.

A Prison Wedding

Some of Ramirez's female admirers began to visit him in San Francisco. Ramirez enjoyed the attention. One of those women was Doreen Lioy, a freelance magazine editor from Burbank, California. Lioy started writing Ramirez in 1985, shortly after he was arrested and waiting for trial in jail.

Lioy said that she felt a connection to Ramirez after seeing his picture on television. Soon she started visiting Ramirez in jail. When he was moved to San Quentin, Lioy continued to visit multiple times per week.

In 1988, Ramirez proposed to Lioy from behind bars, and she accepted. The couple was married in 1996 at San Quentin. Lioy gave Ramirez a platinum wedding band because Satanists do not wear gold. Several members of Ramirez's family attended the wedding, including his brother, sister, and niece. No one from Lioy's family attended the wedding, as they strongly objected.

After their wedding, Lioy continued to support her husband. She declared her enduring love for Ramirez and her belief in his innocence. "He's kind, he's funny, he's charming," she said in 1997. "I think he's really a great person. He's my best friend; he's my buddy."[3] Over the years, however, Lioy's belief in Ramirez appeared to waver. In 2009, DNA evidence linked Ramirez to the 1984 rape and murder of a nine-year-old girl in San Francisco. After that, Lioy never commented publicly on her relationship with Ramirez.

MURDER OF MEI LEUNG

In 2009, DNA evidence tied Richard Ramirez to the 1984 sexual assault and murder of nine-year-old Mei Leung in San Francisco. The young girl was found dead in the basement of her apartment building. She had been beaten, sexually assaulted, and stabbed. Ramirez was known to be living nearby at the time of Leung's murder. Police compared a sample of Ramirez's DNA with evidence found at the crime scene and determined they were a match.

Appeals

Ramirez's lawyers began the appeals process soon after their client's conviction and sentencing in Los Angeles. A defendant sentenced to death in California is granted an automatic, direct appeal to the California Supreme Court. A California capital conviction, in which the defendant is sentenced to death, can also be appealed to federal courts.

Attorney Geraldine Russell from San Diego, California, took the lead on Ramirez's appeals. Russell argued that

Lioy departed the prison after her 1996 wedding alongside prison guards, members of the media, and author Philip Carlo, *left*, who was writing a book about the Night Stalker.

her client should be granted a new trial because Daniel Hernandez and Arturo Hernandez did not adequately represent him. "There were many major mistakes, the least of which was incompetent counsel. [Ramirez's lawyers] should have never been allowed to represent anyone in a capital case," said Russell.[4] In the appeal, Ramirez also claimed that the court made a mistake by not giving him a complete psychiatric evaluation before trial.

The appeals process, especially in a death penalty case like Ramirez's, can take many years or even decades. Ramirez's appeal moved very slowly because there were so many records and transcripts from the trial that needed to be reviewed. The trial record was more than 48,000 pages and took almost ten years to compile and certify as accurate.[5]

It also took several years to find a qualified lawyer to represent Ramirez on appeal and prepare more than 900 pages of written arguments for the appeal. Once the California Supreme Court had the case, it spent 2.5 years deliberating before issuing a decision.[6]

In August 2006, the California Supreme Court rejected Ramirez's first round of appeals. The court upheld his convictions and death sentence. In September, it denied Ramirez's request for a rehearing. However, Ramirez still had a pending legal challenge asserting that California's death penalty was unconstitutional. If that challenge were rejected, the process still would not be finished. Ramirez and his lawyers would be able to spend many more years appealing his conviction and death sentence in federal courts.

Illness and Death

As he continued to file appeals related to his conviction and death sentence, Ramirez was diagnosed with B-cell lymphoma. Lymphoma is a type of blood cancer that affects the body's germ-fighting lymphatic system. He also suffered from a hepatitis C viral infection, which he most likely acquired because of his long history of intravenous drug use. Ramirez experienced various other health effects from these years of chronic substance use.

In early June 2013, 53-year-old Ramirez was taken from San Quentin to Marin General Hospital in Greenbrae, California. On June 7, 2013, he died from complications related to lymphoma. No one from Ramirez's family, including Lioy, claimed his body.

"To me, he had a better death than all those people whose lives he took."[7]

–Reyna Pinon, wife of one of the men who captured Ramirez

Legacy and Impact

Richard Ramirez, the Night Stalker, terrorized California during his crime spree in the mid-1980s. During the long, hot summer of 1985, people lived in fear as the police attempted to identify the serial killer. Disjointed efforts between different police departments and jurisdictions slowed the investigation. Eventually, law enforcement would take the lessons learned from this case to improve future investigations.

The Night Stalker's gruesome crimes have lived on in multiple books, movies, and documentaries. In 2021, streaming service Netflix released a four-part documentary called *Night Stalker: The Hunt for a Serial Killer*. The documentary follows the search for Ramirez. Much of the series is told from the point of view of Frank Salerno and Gil Carrillo, the homicide detectives on the case. "The four-part series is a powerful and haunting

A POTENTIAL PARTNER

Richard Ramirez was accused of acting alone in multiple murders, rapes, and other crimes. In 2016, however, San Francisco police chief Greg Suhr revealed that there is evidence that Ramirez may have had a partner in at least one murder. Suhr explained that a handkerchief found near one of the crime scenes contained bodily fluids of Ramirez and another man. It also had traces of the victim's blood.

addition to the streamer's onslaught of true-crime fare, but more than that, it deftly captures a place and time that many Angelenos will remember as part of their collective history," said Lorraine Ali, a television critic for the *Los Angeles Times*.[8]

For months, Ramirez carried out a string of brutal murders and attacks. Many people who crossed paths with the serial killer believe that he embodied true evil. However, law enforcement's hard work and persistence eventually brought Ramirez to justice.

ESSENTIAL FACTS

TIMELINE

1960: Ricardo "Richard" Ramirez is born in El Paso, Texas, to Julian and Mercedes Ramirez.

1973: Ramirez witnesses his cousin Mike Ramirez fatally shoot his wife in the face.

June 1984: Ramirez breaks into the home of 79-year-old Jennie Vincow and murders her with a knife.

Mar. 1985: Ramirez attacks Maria Hernandez and kills Dayle Okazaki and Veronica Yu on March 17. Around March 28, he murders Vincent and Maxine Zazzara.

May to Aug. 1985: Ramirez commits multiple murders, rapes, and robberies across Southern California.

Aug. 1985: Ramirez travels to San Francisco, where he murders Peter Pan and assaults his wife, Barbara. Ramirez is later spotted driving a stolen orange Toyota by 13-year-old James Romero in Mission Viejo.

Aug. 30–31, 1985: Police announce they have identified Richard Ramirez as the Night Stalker. The next day, angry citizens capture Ramirez in Los Angeles. Police arrive and arrest him.

Jan. 1989: The trial of Richard Ramirez in Los Angeles begins.

Sept. 20, 1989: The jury finds Ramirez guilty on all charges. He is sentenced to death on November 7.

Nov. 1989: Ramirez is transferred to San Quentin State Prison to serve his sentence on death row.

June 7, 2013: Richard Ramirez dies from complications of lymphoma.

IMPACT ON SOCIETY

Richard Ramirez, the Night Stalker, terrorized California during his crime spree in the mid-1980s. Residents, particularly in the Los Angeles area, were gripped with fear. Intense media coverage that often sensationalized the crimes helped heighten the public's fear and panic. People were afraid to go out at night, and many took extra efforts to secure their homes and protect themselves. Once Ramirez was captured, the public breathed a collective sigh of relief.

The Night Stalker case led to changes in law enforcement practices. The case highlighted the importance of cooperation between the public and law enforcement. It also showed the importance of cooperation across police departments and jurisdictions. Law enforcement agencies across the country reevaluated their procedures to apprehend dangerous suspects. They also reexamined the use of technology in criminal investigations.

QUOTE

"It was difficult to believe one man was responsible for everything, since no one in criminal history had been documented doing what Richard did."

—*Detective Gil Carrillo*

GLOSSARY

abduction
The act of taking someone without their consent.

abscess
An area of the body with a buildup of pus caused by an infection.

appeal
A legal proceeding submitted to ask a higher court to review the decision of a lower court.

arraignment
A defendant's first court appearance, in which a judge formally announces a person's charges.

autopsy
An examination of a body to determine cause of death.

ballistics
The science of projectiles and firearms.

beeper
A portable device that makes a noise or vibrates to alert its owner to an incoming message; also called a pager.

caliber
The diameter of the inside of a gun barrel.

casing
In ammunition, the sleeve that contains the gunpowder and bullet.

composite
Made up from different parts or pieces.

decay
To rot or decompose.

epilepsy
A brain disorder that causes seizures.

intravenous
Using or through the veins.

motion
A formal request for a desired ruling, order, or judgment in court.

oral hygiene
The practice of keeping the mouth and teeth clean.

plea
A defendant's formal answer to charges in court.

prosecutor
A lawyer who leads the case against a defendant in court.

ransack
To search in a damaging way for items to steal.

ADDITIONAL RESOURCES

SELECTED BIBLIOGRAPHY

Carlo, Philip. *The Night Stalker: The Life and Crimes of Richard Ramirez*. Citadel, 2016.

Chen, Edwin. "Ramirez Guilty on All Night Stalker Murder Charges." *Los Angeles Times*, 21 Sept. 1989, latimes.com. Accessed 13 Mar. 2024.

Learish, Jessica. "Richard Ramirez: The Story, the Evidence, the Night Stalker." *CBS News*, 21 May 2021, cbsnews.com. Accessed 12 Mar. 2024.

FURTHER READINGS

Cooper, Chris. *Forensic Science*. DK, 2020.

Morris, Rebecca. *Joseph James DeAngelo: The Golden State Killer*. Abdo, 2025.

Newquist, H. P. *Scene of the Crime: Tracking Down Criminals with Forensic Science*. Viking, 2021.

ONLINE RESOURCES

To learn more about serial killers, please visit **abdobooklinks.com** or scan this QR code. These links are routinely monitored and updated to provide the most current information available.

MORE INFORMATION

For more information on this subject, contact or visit the following organizations:

AMERICAN ACADEMY OF FORENSIC SCIENCES (AAFS)

410 N. 21st St.
Colorado Springs, CO 80904
aafs.org

The AAFS is a professional society dedicated to promoting forensic science education and improving accuracy and precision in forensic science.

LOS ANGELES COUNTY SHERIFF'S DEPARTMENT

211 W. Temple St.
Los Angeles, CA 90012
lasd.org

The website of the Los Angeles County Sheriff's Department includes information about the law enforcement agency's work today.

SAN QUENTIN REHABILITATION CENTER

100 Main St.
San Quentin, CA 94964
cdcr.ca.gov/facility-locator/sq/

San Quentin Rehabilitation Center (formerly San Quentin State Prison) is a correctional facility in California where many infamous criminals have been held.

SOURCE NOTES

CHAPTER 1. A KILLING SPREE BEGINS
1. "'Night Stalker' Survivor Picks Out Ramirez in Courtroom." *Los Angeles Times*, 12 Mar. 1986, latimes.com. Accessed 24 June 2024.
2. "Survivor Picks Out Ramirez."
3. "Survivor Picks Out Ramirez."
4. Philip Carlo. *The Night Stalker: The Life and Crimes of Richard Ramirez*. Citadel, 2016. 22.

CHAPTER 2. A VIOLENT HOME
1. Aurelio Rojas and K. Mack Sisk. "Richard Ramirez' 'Highway to Hell.'" *UPI*, 7 Sept. 1985, upi.com. Accessed 24 June 2024.
2. Philip Carlo. *The Night Stalker: The Life and Crimes of Richard Ramirez*. Citadel, 2016. 162.
3. David Holley. "Recalling Ramirez: Even Friends Didn't Trust Him." *Los Angeles Times*, 8 Sept. 1985, latimes.com. Accessed 24 June 2024.
4. Rojas and Sisk, "Richard Ramirez' 'Highway to Hell.'"
5. Carlo, *The Night Stalker*, 173–174.
6. Holley, "Recalling Ramirez."
7. "Heavy Metal, Satanism and the Night Stalker." *UPI*, 2 Sept. 1985, upi.com. Accessed 24 June 2024.

CHAPTER 3. ESCALATING VIOLENCE
1. Samson Amore and Beatrice Verhoeven. "'Night Stalker': Who Was Frank Salerno, the Detective Who Helped Catch Richard Ramirez?" *Wrap*, 15 Jan. 2021, thewrap.com. Accessed 24 June 2024.
2. Philip Carlo. *The Night Stalker: The Life and Crimes of Richard Ramirez*. Citadel, 2016. 35.
3. Gina Tron. "What Made a Young Detective Realize That a Range of Seemingly Random Crimes Were the Work of the 'Night Stalker?'" *Oxygen*, 21 Jan. 2021, oxygen.com. Accessed 24 June 2024.
4. Leo Duran and A Martínez. "This Rookie Had a Hunch about Who the 'Night Stalker' Was, but It Was Hard to Believe." *LAist*, 2 Feb. 2021, laist.com. Accessed 24 June 2024.
5. Carlo, *The Night Stalker*, 69–70.

CHAPTER 4. A CITY GRIPPED BY FEAR
1. Carol McGraw and David Freed. "Law Enforcement Aided by Public: Search for the Stalker—Unity Born of Fear." *Los Angeles Times*, 8 Sept. 1985, latimes.com. Accessed 24 June 2024.
2. Andrea Park. "What Happened to Detective Gil Carrillo from 'Night Stalker?'" *Marie Claire*, 15. Jan. 2021, marieclaire.com. Accessed 24 June 2024.

3. McGraw and Freed, "Law Enforcement Aided by Public."

4. Philip Carlo. *The Night Stalker: The Life and Crimes of Richard Ramirez*. Citadel, 2016. 82.

5. Ellis E. Conklin. "Night Stalker Spreads Terror in Southern California: Sales of Locks, Guns, Burglar Alarms Booming." *UPI*, 31 Aug. 1985, upi.com. Accessed 24 June 2024.

6. Adam Janos. "A Retired L.A. Area Cop on the Community's Terror during the 'Night Stalker" Murders." *A&E*, 5 Oct. 2021, aetv.com. Accessed 24 June 2024.

7. Conklin, "Night Stalker Spreads Terror in Southern California."

CHAPTER 5. ATTACKS IN SAN FRANCISCO

1. Philip Carlo. *The Night Stalker: The Life and Crimes of Richard Ramirez*. Citadel, 2016. 111.

2. Eric Malnic. "Slaying of S.F. Man Linked to Valley Intruder." *Los Angeles Times*, 23 Aug. 1985, latimes.com. Accessed 24 June 2024.

3. Malnic, "Slaying Linked to Valley Intruder."

4. Malnic, "Slaying Linked to Valley Intruder."

5. "Yesterday's Crimes: How Dianne Feinstein Tipped Off the Night Stalker." *SF Weekly*, 17 Mar. 2016, sfweekly.com. Accessed 24 June 2024.

6. "Coast Sheriff Says 14 Killings Linked." *New York Times*, 24 Aug. 1985, nytimes.com. Accessed 24 June 2024.

7. "How Feinstein Tipped Off the Night Stalker."

8. Bianca Buono. "4 Ties the 'Night Stalker' Has to Arizona That You Probably Didn't Know About." *12 News*, 12 Feb. 2021, 12news.com. Accessed 24 June 2024.

CHAPTER 6. A BREAK IN THE CASE

1. "How a 13-Year-Old Boy Helped Capture the 'Night Stalker' Serial Killer." *CBS News*, 19 May 2017, cbsnews.com. Accessed 24 June 2024.

2. Philip Carlo. *The Night Stalker: The Life and Crimes of Richard Ramirez*. Citadel, 2016. 116–118.

3. "Shedding Some Light on the Night Stalker." *San Francisco Examiner*, 13 Dec. 2009, sfexaminer.com. Accessed 24 June 2024.

4. Richard Simon. "Mission Viejo Boy Gets Stalker Bounty." *Los Angeles Times*, 25 Oct. 1989, latimes.com. Accessed 24 June 2024.

SOURCE NOTES CONTINUED

CHAPTER 7. CAPTURING THE KILLER
1. David Freed and Carol McGraw. "Police Identify Stalker Suspect: 25-Year-Old L.A. Man Named in Seven-Month Spree of Killings." *Los Angeles Times*, 31 Aug. 1985, latimes.com. Accessed 24 June 2024.

2. Freed and McGraw, "Police Identify Stalker Suspect."

3. Philip Carlo. *The Night Stalker: The Life and Crimes of Richard Ramirez*. Citadel, 2016. 184–185.

4. Emma Perry and Alex Diaz. "Hero Couple Relive Moment They Ended Night Stalker's Reign of Terror." *Sun*, 25 Jan. 2021, the-sun.com. Accessed 24 June 2024.

5. Yurina Melara Valiulis. "Participant Remembers 'Night Stalker' Richard Ramirez Capture in East LA." *Boyle Heights Beat*, 11 June 2013, boyleheightsbeat.com. Accessed 24 June 2024.

6. David Freed and Carol McGraw. "Citizens Capture Stalker Fugitive." *Los Angeles Times*, 1 Sept. 1985, latimes.com. Accessed 24 June 2024.

7. Russel Snyder. "Police Saturday Arrested the Alleged Night Stalker." *UPI*, 31 Aug. 1985, upi.com. Accessed 24 June 2024.

8. Jessica Learish. "Richard Ramirez: The Story, the Evidence, the Night Stalker." *CBS News*, 21 May 2021, cbsnews.com. Accessed 24 June 2024.

9. Leo Duran and A Martínez. "This Rookie Had a Hunch about Who the 'Night Stalker' Was, but It Was Hard to Believe." *LAist*, 2 Feb. 2021, laist.com. Accessed 24 June 2024.

10. Freed and McGraw, "Citizens Capture Stalker Fugitive."

CHAPTER 8. TRIAL AND CONVICTION
1. Robert W. Stewart. "Stalker Suspect Ramirez Charged in 13 More Deaths." *Los Angeles Times*, 28 Sept. 1985, latimes.com. Accessed 24 June 2024.

2. Marcia Chambers. "Defendant in 'Night Stalker' Case Denies Killing 14 in California." *New York Times*, 25 Oct. 1985, nytimes.com. Accessed 24 June 2024.

3. Barbara Jones. "Night Stalker Conviction Capped Four-Year Legal Saga." *Sun* [San Bernardino, CA], 7 June 2013, sbsun.com. Accessed 24 June 2024.

4. Edwin Chen. "Jurors Begin to Hear Grim Tale of Alleged Night Stalker Crimes." *Los Angeles Times*, 31 Jan. 1989, latimes.com. Accessed 24 June 2024.

5. Jessica Learish. "Richard Ramirez: The Story, the Evidence, the Night Stalker." *CBS News*, 21 May 2021, cbsnews.com. Accessed 24 June 2024.

6. Edwin Chen. "Defense Faces a Wealth of Evidence in Stalker Case." *Los Angeles Times*, 17 Apr. 1989, latimes.com. Accessed 24 June 2024.

7. Chen, "Defense Faces Wealth of Evidence."

8. Jerry Hicks. "Victim of Horror Finally Speaks." *Los Angeles Times*, 12 Oct. 1989, latimes.com. Accessed 24 June 2024.

9. Michael D. Harris. "Defense Rests in Night Stalker Trial." *UPI*, 20 June 1989, upi.com. Accessed 24 June 2024.

10. Trish Long. "'Night Stalker' Case Goes to Jury." *El Paso Times*, 27 July 1989, elpasotimes.com. Accessed 24 June 2024.

11. Long, "'Night Stalker' Case Goes to Jury."

12. Edwin Chen. "Ramirez Guilty on All Night Stalker Murder Charges." *Los Angeles Times*, 21 Sept. 1989, latimes.com. Accessed 24 June 2024.

13. Michael D. Harris. "'Night Stalker' Sentenced to Gas Chamber." *UPI*, 7 Nov. 1989, upi.com. Accessed 24 June 2024.

14. Paul Buchanan. "How a 13-Year-Old Boy Brought Down L.A.'s Most Notorious Serial Killer." *Los Angeles Magazine*, 15 May 2017, lamag.com. Accessed 24 June 2024.

15. Harris, "'Night Stalker' Sentenced to Gas Chamber."

16. Jerry Hicks. "Concern for Victims Prompts O.C. to Drop Case against Ramirez." *Los Angeles Times*, 9 Nov. 1989, latimes.com. Accessed 24 June 2024.

CHAPTER 9. LIFE AND DEATH BEHIND BARS

1. Philip Carlo. *The Night Stalker: The Life and Crimes of Richard Ramirez*. Citadel, 2016. 408.

2. "Governor Gavin Newsom Orders a Halt to the Death Penalty in California." *Governor Gavin Newsom*, 13 Mar. 2019, gov.ca.gov. Accessed 24 June 2024.

3. Andrea Park. "Where Is Doreen Lioy, Wife of 'Night Stalker' Richard Ramirez, Now?" *Marie Claire*, 13 Jan. 2021, marieclaire.com. Accessed 24 June 2024.

4. Carlo, *The Night Stalker*, 419.

5. Maura Dolan. "State High Court Rejects 'Night Stalker's' Appeal." *Los Angeles Times*, 8 Aug. 2006, latimes.com. Accessed 24 June 2024.

6. Dolan, "Court Rejects Appeal."

7. Rong-Gong Lin II, Hector Becerra, and Steve Chawkins. "For Some of Richard Ramirez's Victims, a Bitter Look Back." *Los Angeles Times*, 7 June 2013, latimes.com. Accessed 24 June 2024.

8. Lorraine Ali. "Review: Relive the Terrifying Summer of '85 with Netflix's Haunting 'Night Stalker' Series." *Los Angeles Times*, 13 Jan. 2021, latimes.com. Accessed 24 June 2024.

INDEX

Abowath, Elyas, 47
Abowath, Sakina, 47
appeals, 94–97
Arnold, Judy, 42–43
arrests, 19, 50, 65, 68, 76–77
Arthur, Linda, 36
autopsies, 9, 24

ballistics, 9, 11, 25, 44, 53, 81
Bell, Mabel "Ma," 30, 63
Bennett, Whitney, 31, 33
Block, Sherman, 38, 54, 66–68,
Boese, Darlene, 28
Broussard, John, 51
burglaries, 21, 31, 43, 49, 51, 61, 78, 80, 83
bus terminals, 24, 61, 69–70, 83

California Supreme Court, 94, 96
Cannon, Mary Louise, 31
Carns, Bill, 57–58, 89
Carrillo, Gil, 7–11, 24–30, 33–34, 36–39, 40–41, 43, 44, 49–50, 52, 54, 58, 65, 76–77, 98
Clark, Ray, 84, 87
courtroom security, 80

De La Torre, Angelina, 74–75
De La Torre, Manuel, 75
Doi, William "Bill," 29, 61
drug use, 19, 20–21, 24, 67, 97
Duenas, Joseph, 7

El Paso, Texas, 12, 17, 19, 20, 61, 63, 65, 67, 84
Elder, Jon, 38–39
epilepsy, 14, 15
Erickson, Inez, 57–58, 89

Feinstein, Dianne, 52–55
fingerprints, 8, 11, 28, 33, 40–41, 59, 60, 65, 81, 83, 84

Gallegos, Jorge, 6–7
Golden Gate Bridge, 55
Gregg, Earl, Jr., 21

Halpin, Phil, 78, 81, 87
heavy metal music, 20, 21, 63, 69
Hernandez, Arturo, 78–79, 84–87, 96
Hernandez, Daniel, 78–79, 84–87, 96
Hernandez, Maria, 4–6, 8–9, 26, 34, 44
Higgins, Patty, 81

identification of Night Stalker, 65, 66–68

Khovananth, Chainarong, 43–44, 83
Khovananth, Somkid, 43–44
Klotz, Carl, 49–50
Kneiding, Lela, 42–43, 44
Kneiding, Max, 42–43, 44
Kyle, Carol, 31, 34, 44

Lang, Florence "Nettie," 30
Leung, Mei, 94
Leung, Peter, 42
Lioy, Doreen, 93–94, 97
Loftus, Elizabeth, 86
Los Angeles County Sheriff's Department, 7, 25, 27, 29, 36, 38, 40–43, 51, 58, 61
Los Angeles Police Department (LAPD), 40–41, 44, 46, 50, 67, 70, 76

Martin, Glynn, 46
Meyers, Donna, 62–63
Monterey Park, California, 4, 6, 9, 25, 28–29, 36–38, 61
Munoz, Luis, 74

Nelson, Joyce, 36–39
Night Stalker: The Hunt for a Serial Killer, 98–99

Okazaki, Dayle, 4, 6, 8–9, 11, 24–25, 44
oral health, 19–20, 26, 29, 34, 41, 42, 43, 61, 63, 68, 76, 86

Pan, Barbara, 48–50, 53–54, 62, 63, 92
Pan, Peter, 48–50, 53–54, 62, 63, 92
Perez, Jesse, 61, 65
Petersen, Chris, 46–47
Petersen, Virginia, 46–47
Polo, Bruno, 22

Ramirez, Andres, 78
reward money, 53, 62
Robles, Carmello, 72–73
Rodriguez, Armando, 63
Rodriguez, John, 39
Romero, James, 56–58
Russell, Geraldine, 94–96

Salerno, Frank, 11, 25, 26–28, 33, 34, 39–44, 49–52, 54, 58, 65, 76, 98
San Francisco, California, 21, 48–55, 56, 62–63, 78, 90, 92–93, 94, 98
San Francisco Police Department, 50, 98

San Quentin State Prison, 90–93, 97
Santoro, Joe, 37–38
Satanism, 19, 21, 24, 30, 43, 47, 52, 58, 61, 63, 79, 90, 93
sentencing, 88–89
shoe prints, 23–24, 26, 29, 30, 32, 33, 36, 38, 39, 42, 44, 52, 54–55, 81–83
Singletary, Phyllis, 88
sketch artists, 9, 34, 44, 53, 63
Smith, J. D., 23–24, 28
Solano, Felipe, 61–62
stolen cars, 40–41, 50, 57–59
Suhr, Greg, 98

Torres, Paul, 29–30
trials, 78–89
Tucson, Arizona, 69–70
Tynan, Michael, 80, 89

Uloth, Ross, 23–24, 28

Vietnam War, 14–15, 38
Villanueva, Manuela, 72
Vincow, Jennie, 28

Yu, Tsai-Lian "Veronica," 7, 9, 11, 24–25, 44

Zazzara, Maxine, 22–26, 83
Zazzara, Vincent, 22–26, 83

ABOUT THE AUTHOR

CARLA MOONEY

Carla Mooney is a graduate of the University of Pennsylvania. Today, she writes for young people and is the author of many books for young adults and children. Mooney enjoys reading about true crime and investigations.